EMOTION AND SPIRIT

Questioning the Claims
of Psychoanalysis and Religion

Neville Symington

with a new Preface by the author

Foreword by
Jon Stokes

London
KARNAC BOOKS

First published in 1994 by Cassell

Reprinted in 1998, by arrangement
with Neville Symington, by
H. Karnac (Books) Ltd.
58 Gloucester Road
London SW7 4QY

British Library Cataloguing in Publication Data
A C.I.P. record for this book is available from the British Library.
  ISBN 1 85575 203 4

Edited, designed, and produced by Communication Crafts

Printed in Great Britain by BPC Wheatons Ltd, Exeter

10 9 8 7 6 5 4 3 2 1

Contents

Emotion and spirit

Preface

I am pleased at the opportunity to write a preface to *Emotion and Spirit* afforded by this new printing, four years after it was first published. It is not the best known of my books, but it is the one that cost more blood and sweat than any other because it forced me to think more than any other book has done. My compensation for this effort was the significant number of people who have written to me to say that it has had a transforming effect on their lives. I had similar letters when my book on narcissism was published the year before.* One person wrote:

> The book had a dramatic effect on me. It cracked open a bit of pathology which had held me in its grip for nearly twenty years. . . .

This raises the question: what in these two books is responsible for this impact? I believe it is that both books aim to single out those elements in our interior lives that obstruct our fulfilment as persons. To achieve this fulfilment, we need the understanding of our inner lives that has come to us both through psychoanalysis and also through the central insights of the great religious traditions of the world. It is more than just a conceptual matter; it is also the form in which insights are expressed. An insight will not make an impact if it is embedded in a background that is alien to the tonality of our emotions. In fact, a different background changes the emotional impact altogether. I am certain that the language of authentic religious experience does touch the soul whereas that of positivistic science does not, but I am not here just manipulating language for the sake of

---

*Symington, N., *Narcissism: A New Theory*. London: Karnac Books, 1993.

effect. Rather, it is my conviction that the religious or libertarian model is the one that corresponds most closely to the lived experience of human beings.

There is one misconception that I should like to clear up. I have made a distinction here between primitive and mature religion, and I have—in the way that I have expressed myself—given reason for people to think that the division is between the religions of uncivilized races and those religions of high culture, Western and Eastern. I could have approached the matter in a different way and separated the genuine mysticism existent in all religions from the institutional forms that frequently embody a religious typology that attempts reparation through external sacrificial acts. Mature religion aims at transformation of the mind and heart, whereas what I have referred to as primitive religion is concerned with external and placatory acts that do not intend to transform the heart. The point I want to emphasize here is that primitive forms of religion are found in religions of all types and that mysticism is also found in religions of all kinds. What I have referred to as the core religious insights are to be found in religious traditions of all kinds. It would be wrong, however, to think that all religious traditions are equal in their mystical endowment. Some clearly have a richer seam of mysticism than others, but the point I want to make is that what appears primitive may be more richly endowed with mystical insight than one that appears culturally sophisticated.

The other matter I want to address briefly here is the language that some have found objectionable. In particular, people have objected to my use of the words *moral, virtue,* and *spiritual.* One reviewer said,

> I find the term 'spirituality' too laden with excess Judaeo-Christian baggage to be suitable.

I was faced with two choices: either to invent new words, or to try to invest these words with their true meaning. I am quite aware that 'moral' is often read as 'moralistic', 'virtue' as 'hypocrisy', and 'spiritual' as 'scorning the world', but these are perversions of their true meaning. I want to restore to these words their true meaning, and I address the reader thus:

> 'Look, there is a religion quite free of magic and superstition, and words such as *spiritual, moral,* and *virtue* are ones that we

need if we are to help people achieve emotional strength, a sense of purpose, and confidence.'

Many psychoanalysts and mental health workers misuse the adjective 'moral'. They refer to someone as being moral when in fact the appropriate word is 'moralistic'. People behave *morally* when an inner decision to follow conscience guides them to what is right rather than to what is wrong; people are *moralistic* when they attribute with contempt base motives to others or to themselves. So, also, many think that 'virtuous' is synonymous with 'self-righteous'. Virtue comes from the Latin *virtus*—strength—and means the inner emotional strength that endows someone with courage and confidence. The mistake is to confuse what is inner with what is outer. I wonder whether these misconceptions are signs that many of us are out of contact with our inner emotional acts?

I can see the arguments in favour of inventing new words—that it is so difficult to purge ourselves of the excess of 'Judaeo–Christian baggage', as the reviewer says. (I think it should be noted that what the reviewer refers to as 'Judaeo–Christian baggage' is again a selection from that tradition of what is made up of magic and superstition and a neglect of the mystical.) Purging ourselves of false meanings is such a long process that it might be better to invent new words. I respect this view, and there is obviously a great deal to be said for it, yet the more difficult path is not necessarily the more advisable. Spiritual writers are fond of making an analogy between the planting of vines and the spiritual endeavour. The best wine comes from the most inhospitable soil, and so, too, what is of great value is usually achieved only with time, struggle, and patience.

I can see a very strong reason for re-investing words with their true and ancient meaning: to make clear when we are talking of the same mental processes that have been described by mystics and spiritual writers, as opposed to when we are in possession of something new, something that was not known and understood by them. One of the points of this book is to highlight the fact that psychoanalysis brought a radically new understanding to emotional life. When Melanie Klein opened a door and pointed to the 'inner world', she was talking of the soul that had been the concern of spiritual writers since 500 BC, but when she began to describe part-objects, splitting, and projective and introjective processes she was in possession of new knowledge—knowledge that the Buddha or John of the Cross did not know about or had not formulated into a set of principles. Only when it is clear exactly what is new about psychoanalysis can it be used properly and be a potent force. Therefore, it is necessary to distinguish what is new from what is old, to invent new words for new realities, and to keep old words for what is already known and has been described in the past.

The other criticism that has been voiced by a few is the absence of Bion. I think this is entirely valid, and it is one of the book's defects. I shall not bother to explain why I left him out. The serious reader is interested in the subject matter, not my pathology. Another fault of the book, which is not unrelated to the absence of Bion, is the failure to supply an ontological foundation for natural religion. It is adumbrated in the section on the spirituality of the Upanishads, but the brevity of this in the book may lead the reader to underestimate its importance. The link between the insights of the Upanishads and the philosophy of Spinoza has not been made. These four factors—Bion, ontology, the Upanishads, and Spinoza—will receive more attention in a book under preparation.

* * *

It is my hope that *Emotion and Spirit* may awaken curiosity in this domain of experience. Without the core values of religion, emotional life is destitute; without understanding the way in which the emotions operate, these values will remain antiquarian oddities. There is a malaise in modern culture. I believe that this can change only if emotional life becomes permeated with religion's core values. This book aims to bring the two elements of this marriage into more general consciousness. In this, I believe, lies hope.

September 1998

Foreword

Jon Stokes
Director, Tavistock Consultancy Service

Religion and psychoanalysis are two fields of human endeavour that have not often had much good to say about each other. However, there are certainly some striking similarities. Both make a similar claim to an ultimate truth—that it is the capacity to achieve and maintain a relationship with 'the good object' that results in emotional or spiritual maturity. For the psychoanalyst, this is a scientifically demonstrable truth; for the religious, it is based on intuitive understanding. Both offer 'ways' to personal salvation.

Both religion and psychoanalysis enable us as individuals to pursue the quest for truth through shedding light on who and how we currently are in deeper ways than we are immediately aware—and on what we have become without necessarily realizing it. Both provide inter-personal settings specifically structured to permit the revelation of spiritual or emotional truths. Neville Symington, who has studied philosophy and theology and has for many years now been a practising psychoanalyst, is well placed to examine the ways in which these two creations of the human mind might more profitably contribute to each other's further development.

Writings on religion cover a wide range of subjects. These include the Mystical: the exploration of mystical experiences and beliefs in the supernatural; the Moral: religion as a system of core values; and the Spiritual: the place of detachment and of the process of reflection in human development.

When this book was first published, it was criticized in some quarters because of a misunderstanding about the focus of its argument. Symington's concern is not so much with any comparisons there may be between organized religion and organized psychoanalysis or with religion as a set of mystical beliefs, it is with a better understanding of a field of shared interest to both religious and psychoanalyst—the relationship between the moral dimension of the mind and the emotional or spiritual health of the individual. The link is the state of the internalized relationship to 'the good'. In religious terms, there is a spiritual quest involved in the psychoanalytic task of attempting to discover the true intentional base of one's actions, both good and bad. This requires a capacity and space for reflection that the practices of both religion and psychoanalysis endeavour to provide.

The practise of both religion and psychoanalysis can degenerate at times into, for example, a bludgeoning moralizing of the individual, as opposed to assisting in the development of a moral sense. There are, of course, a plethora of psychoanalytic 'faiths' around the world, but this is not simply so much further evidence of irrational group behaviour but because the truths that psychoanalysis works at are of the most profound 'spiritual' significance and provoke the most vehement of debate. For Symington, religion at its best is an institution 'whose goal is the good', a set of core values and methods that provide opportunities to reflect on the significance of one's actions for oneself and others . The psychoanalytic experience provides something similar, but whereas religions have an articulated set of core values, these are, Symington argues, largely implicit but nevertheless essential to the theory and practice of psychoanalysis.

Freud, of course, was a vehement critic of religion, which he saw as involving a state of mind inimical to the search for scientific truth. However, subsequent developments, particularly those within the British School of psychoanalysis by Melanie Klein and Donald Winnicott, made a moral dimension within the theory of psychoanalysis more explicit. Mental health depends on a capacity and willingness to acknowledge and make reparation for destructive impulses and acts, as well as on creative and life instincts. The two domains of moral truth and scientific truth which became separated by the Enlightenment during the course of the seventeenth century are again brought into conjunction by these developments in psychoanalysis.

Further theoretical developments, particularly by Wilfred Bion, on how the capacity for discerning right from wrong in a scientific sense in the external world is dependent on the capacity for sustaining a distinction and making a choice between 'the good object' and the 'the bad object' in the internal world, have profound implications.

Psychological development rests on the capacity for bearing sometimes painful emotional truths, which in turn require moral decisions
about how one treats or acts towards others. This is, in religious terminology, the domain of the spiritual.

In this book, Symington argues for a distinction between primitive
and mature religions. The former are preoccupied by the paranoid–
schizoid demands of the survival instinct, whereas mature religions
are interested in the transcendence of this fact. However, it does so
generally by having detachment from any erotic ties or attachments as
its highest ideal, which is expressed through the rules governing the
lives of its priesthood. Psychoanalysis believes the reverse—that only
through making and sustaining attachments that necessarily involve
an erotic element is it possible to pursue 'the good' and hence the
truth. This is expressed succinctly in Keats' statement of his fundamental sustaining belief in 'the truth of the imagination and the
holiness of the heart's affections'.

One of the causes of the current 'crisis' in psychoanalysis is its
difficulty communicating its wisdom to a significant audience beyond
the helping professions, which is a difficulty not dissimilar to the
uncertainties surrounding existing forms of religious institution.
Psychoanalysis, unlike religion, does not have institutional forms—
beyond either the clinical setting or the training institute—that
enable people to work collectively at its subject matter. Although the
group relations work developed originally by the Tavistock is one attempt to develop such methods of enquiry, it has largely been ignored
by psychoanalysts.

Symington makes the daring proposal that dialogue with those
from the conventionally religious field might assist in the further development of the theory and practise of psychoanalysis. Those drawn
to religion and those to psychoanalysis as sources of profound truth
could, in Symington's argument, assist each other's explorations of
the related domains of spiritual and emotional development.

In the early years of the development of psychoanalysis, psychoanalysts—for example, in the British school, Roger Money-Kyrle,
Donald Winnicott, and Wilfred Bion himself—did not shy away from
attempting to apply the profound claims of their theories to the wider
world. With some notable exceptions, psychoanalysts have tended in
more recent years to focus inevitably on the detail of certain technical
and theoretical matters. This concentration has involved a retreat
from the wider world, a retreat that is a contributing factor to the

current difficulties facing psychoanalysis. Symington is unusual in not shying away from the heat and inevitable controversy that any attempt to speak to larger questions and larger audiences about how human beings live their lives outside the consulting-room will produce. In inviting a dialogue between religion and psychoanalysis, Neville Symington is endeavouring to restore the spirit to psychoanalysis.

September 1998

Acknowledgements

While writing this book I have pressed various chapters upon colleagues to solicit their comments and opinion. I should like to thank Nina Coltart who read the chapter on Hinduism and Buddhism and pointed out some lacunae which I have made good. I should like to thank her also for the encouragement that she has given me to continue investigating this subject over the past few years. I want to thank Louis Zinkin for kindly reading the chapter on Jung and sending me his comments and, along with many others, I was saddened at his sudden death so shortly after. I should like to thank Dennis Duncan for reading the chapter on the Judaeo-Christian tradition and also for his warm encouragement, and Doris McIlwain for reading the chapter on Meissner and making valuable suggestions. I also want to thank David Roderick for kindly obtaining for me references to books about psychoanalysis by religious authors.

I also want to thank Mrs Isca Wittenberg for going to trouble to get me information on Judaism but more particularly for participating in many discussions about the relation between psychoanalysis and religion and for her conviction that psychoanalysis lacked a dimension which only religion could provide. The conversations I had with her and the exchanges of letters on this subject have been invaluable. She always did me the honour of offering frank criticism where it was appropriate. She has thus contributed significantly to the book as also to my own development.

I want to thank Judith Longman whose personal interest in the book has gone beyond the call of duty. Without her interest and determination this book would not have been written or published. I would also like to thank David Black for first suggesting that I attempt to write a book on this subject.

I want to thank Bob Gosling who, when I was working as one of his staff at the Tavistock, first prodded me into integrating my religious and psychoanalytic insights. He and his wife's friendship to my wife and me since then has been an encouragement to pursue this study.

I should also like to thank Guy Braithwaite. The long discussions we had together on the relations between the religious and secular world have had their influence in this book. I would also like to thank Patrick Carey and his family whose kindness in a time of crisis allowed deeper thoughts to mature.

Then I want to thank three old friends. It was deep and long conversations with them many years ago that sowed the seeds of what has many years later emerged in this book. As long ago as 1965 I had long conversations with John Perry which deepened my understanding of religion and human nature, and more recently he has been good enough to read with care the chapter on the Judaeo-Christian tradition and put me right on some significant points. His very individual understanding of scripture has always been a source of inspiration. Then I want to thank Bill McSweeney whose personal help and friendship allowed me to focus on what is central in human endeavour. In darker times he shone a light into areas of religious significance. Then I want to thank Richard Champion who, in the midst of bubbling fun, has always had that rare gift of seeing what was essential and dismissing the insignificant. Friendship with all three of them helped me to forge an understanding of religion that was emotionally significant and gave me a vision that has deepened with the years. I would also like to thank Charles Davis, who in his time was a mentor to all of us and whose inspiration altered the inner and outer direction of our lives.

I should also like to thank my wife, Joan, for her considerable patience in the face of the ever-present 'book'. She also read the whole manuscript and told me frankly what made poor sense. She is undoubtedly my best critic and has never been afraid to censor work that is unclear, repetitive or trite. I should also like to thank my two sons, Andrew and David, for the interest they have taken in this book and also for information which they have gathered for me from time to time while I was writing it.

1994

To David

Introduction

This book embodies a personal hypothesis which can be stated quite simply. It is that traditional religion is not relevant to man's manner of living in the modern world. As a consequence, the human sciences are secular and have repudiated the core values of traditional religion. This is particularly so of psychoanalysis which, with Freud as its founder, has explicitly and vehemently abjured religion and all its contents, although the implicit situation is often at odds with this.

Psychoanalysis, however, does inhabit and explicate precisely that place in the world that is relevant to present-day human living: the sphere of emotional action existing between people who live in intimacy with one another. Psychoanalysis has largely failed for the opposite reason: although it inhabits the sphere that is relevant to modern man yet its anthroposophy is woefully inadequate as it does not have answers to questions like, 'What is man's purpose?'; 'What is the meaning of life?'; 'How do man and woman find fulfilment?'

Estranged from these *core values* modern man feels alienated, suffers from meaninglessness and wanders through the world a lost soul. Traditional religions do have answers, and in their essentials these answers, although arrived at by thinkers in different religious traditions, have been and are remarkably similar.

Quite simply, religion and psychoanalysis need each other. Religion needs psychoanalysis so it can begin to exist in the place where the life of modern man is lived. Psychoanalysis needs religion so that it may come into possession of those *core values* which endow life with meaning. However, if the two are to come into a living and fertile relation with one another, each has to renounce much baggage which is extrinsic to their central reality. Traditional religions will need to relinquish many rituals, beliefs and *praxis* which are peripheral to religion and only serve to obscure the *core values*. Psychoanalysis also needs to relinquish much irrelevant theory before it can embrace those *core values*.

The book is presented in four parts. My guiding star is the belief that there is religious truth which can be established through reason, and that it is of immediate practical relevance to each person. Many of us have

1

abandoned belief in traditional religion, replacing it with a dedication to political, philosophic or aesthetic ideals or with a scepticism whose heart is despair. To find meaning in life it is necessary to incorporate the self and other: an interpretation in psychoanalysis is a statement that has meaning for both the patient and the analyst; meaning is a reality that transcends the two and has wider repercussions. In Part One I start by differentiating between *primitive* and *mature* religions, which are key analytical concepts throughout the book. I go on to seek insight into the major traditional religions and then to examine the concept of a *natural religion* before differentiating religion from spirituality and spirituality from morality. I end this section with an attempt to define religion.

In Part Two I examine the psychoanalytic approach to religion. Freud's psychology of religion and Meissner's critique of this are discussed and then Jung's analysis of religion. I then look at the further development of psychoanalysis and religion in later Freudian analysts and end by giving special consideration to the contribution of Erich Fromm.

Part Three considers the human condition that came to consciousness in the light of *mature religions* within civilization. We have in our present-day social scientists, ecologists and social reformers a new breed of preachers. They preach against the exploitation of the Third World by developed countries and the contamination and destruction of the planet, yet there is little evidence of scientific investigation into the inner human structure that gives rise to this shocking state of today's world. There is a wealth of Marxist and neo-Marxist critique but this utterly fails to grasp the inner state of man that brings such human tragedy about. I attempt then to analyse narcissism, the inner structure of which I believe gives the most convincing account of human greed and rapaciousness. Finally, I look at the goal of psychoanalysis, which is the transformation of narcissism. Psychoanalysis shares this goal with all *mature religions*.

In Part Four I elucidate the spiritual function of psychoanalysis, and in particular demonstrate that it is a spirituality-in-the-world, showing that self-knowledge which is a declared aim of psychoanalysis is inseparable from emotional acts of virtue. This I believe will be the most controversial part of the book and I am fearful of being misunderstood. I try to elucidate what I mean by 'emotional action' and the whole section stands or falls upon whether this concept is understood. If it is, then the spiritual import of our inner activities will be obvious; if not, what I have said will only cause annoyance.

The book then is something of a risk. It may be dismissed as the ravings of a crank or for some it may throw light upon the heart of man's religious effort. Time will be the only judge of this.

Introduction

I was given two years in which to write this book. I have a full analytic practice, sit on various professional committees, am required to lecture and give papers and am father in a growing family, so my time for writing in each week is small and for research even less. The task I was given was to produce a book on 'psychoanalysis and religion', a subject so vast that anyone with common sense would not consider attempting such a work in so short a time. I decided however to rise to the challenge because it is a subject which is, I believe, of crucial importance. To write the book would enable me to know the contents of my own mind, as it is only through active communication to the 'other' that I truly come to know myself.

The string that links one chapter to another and one part to another and each part to the whole is the personal hypothesis that psychoanalysis is largely failing to heal those with sick minds because it is devoid of those core values which have been central to all the great religious traditions, and that traditional religions fail in the world of today because they apply their values in a realm which is irrelevant to the modern world. This is the negative side of the picture, but what I try to present is a positive position: that the only religion that is capable of being truly incarnate within the emotional life of human beings is what I have termed *natural religion*. Revealed religion in the West or Eastern religions whose founders have become divinized are, through their estrangement from the locus of human emotions, by their nature hostile to psychoanalysis and vice versa.

I try therefore to present what I mean by natural religion. If I had the mind of a Whitehead then the thesis could be presented succinctly. Bernard Shaw once wrote to *The Times* that he had written a long letter because he did not have the time to write a short one. Such is the character of this book. There is a central theme which is approached from different directions in separate sections of the book. I come at the theme from diverse angles and I hope that the central argument will be clear. This book then represents 'work in progress'. In an art exhibition we frequently come across a painting with the legend beneath 'unfinished' and yet people look at such paintings and find it worthwhile to do so. Such also is the character of this book. It is the outline for the finished product. It is a preliminary sketch. It illustrates the direction of my thinking without working out its consequences in detail. I hope though that others may follow who will enlarge and refine its arguments.

REFERENCE

A. N. Whitehead (1930) *Religion in the Making* (Cambridge University Press).

PART ONE

In this first section I survey some of the key religious themes in order to isolate that kernel which lies at the heart of all the major religious traditions. Most psychoanalytic writings on the subject identify religion with the Judaeo-Christian tradition. Those who do not make this identification frequently emphasize the cultic aspects of religion to the exclusion of its moral and spiritual dimension.

All too often religion is associated with theism, yet the Buddha, according to the Theravada tradition, was one of the most thoroughgoing atheists the world has ever seen but few would deny that he was a religious teacher. I therefore define religion in a way that encompasses religions such as Theravada Buddhism and Taoism which are explicitly atheistic in order to arrive at a definition for which the existence of God is not the central element. There are some definitions of religion that include any ideology, aesthetic or political. Such all-inclusiveness makes the word 'religion' meaningless. I have tried to focus on those elements in which the essence of religion is to be found. Only then is it possible to establish the relationship between psychoanalysis and religion.

1
The Nature of Primitive Religion

If a stone falls and crushes a passer-by, it was an evil spirit that dislodged it: there is no chance about it. If a man is dragged out of his canoe by an alligator, it is because he was bewitched: there is no chance about it. If a warrior is killed or wounded by lance-thrust, it is because he was not in a state to parry the blow, a spell has been cast upon him: there is no chance about it.

(Bergson, 1935)

The primitive mind endows its world with agents. It makes a god or gods the cause of those events which affect man, which may exist in a living individual, or in the ghost of a dead one; they may exist in animals, plants, the sun, or the moon. The idea of spirits inhabiting the natural world of primitive man is familiar to most of us, but what I wish to emphasize is the *source* of such a belief, and how it contributes to the idea of primitive religion.

Animism can only occur when there is a concept of the individual as agent. The animistic world is a projection of the self as agent – the representational self – into the natural world or the imagined natural world.

The *representational self* consists of 'I' and 'I-of-the-Other', myself and my tribe. The tribe and clan of which the individual is a part *is* his world. The Other, my tribe, assumes an inflated importance by virtue of an equivalent devaluation of the outsider. Lienhardt says that the Dinka dwell little on the fancies of any 'other world' of different constitution (p. 28). The inference I make from analytical experience is that this involves an active obliteration of the outside world. The instinct for physical survival in the tribal group is the remote cause that drives this wedge between the familiar and the stranger, creating a split where the one is upgraded and the other degraded. The survival instinct is the remote cause that fashions the motivational direction of the tribe but it is hitched at the same time to a magnification of the tribe's importance. Logically there is no reason why

7

the needs of this tribe, on this side of the river, are to be attended to in preference to any other except that 'I' am a member of this tribe. And why I should endow myself with this preference is not rational but it is a basic assumption of the primitive mentality. This basic assumption, which seems so obvious that it seems foolhardy to question, is precisely the one which was challenged head-on by those teachers who founded *mature religion*. Therefore the instinct for physical survival combined with tribal self-magnification as a motivational force distinguishes primitive from mature religion. Freud cherished some of the values of mature religion, yet did not conceptualize them as having anything to do with religion. What he knew as religion was *primitive religion*. He had therefore a restricted concept of religion.

The notion of primitive religion in the pure state is a logical category and not to be found in reality. In primitive cultures today there is always an admixture of the values of advanced societies. In those races where it flourishes in its purest forms the human effort of the whole group is geared towards survival. The natural environment out of which the tribe scoops its living is its ecological niche; this *is* its world. The 'world' of the tribe is not that of the scientists but one that is fashioned by minds governed by this driving force of the survival instinct. Through instinct the tribe marks out its territory which is the focus of its economic activity. Because the tribe is closely tied in its activity by its survival needs, any unusual event is a potential threat to its environment. Some tribes live perpetually on the brink of a fragile survival which, when threatened, stirs fear. Anything unusual or odd may be an omen of disaster: for example, when a Dinka tribesman saw an unusually large pumpkin, he sacrificed a goat to the *jok* or Power (Lienhardt, 1987). When survival is dependent upon the capricious fortunes of the natural environment any strange or unusual phenomenon is invested with fear. Concerns about other peoples or higher values would sap the energies which are necessary for survival. The primitive mind is focused upon the tangible requirements of survival and when they are threatened the god or gods are invoked. These are located within the tribe's ecological niche, even when the god is located in as universal a phenomenon as the sun which, because it is local, is in the tribe's world. When the primitive mind is enslaved to survival needs, there are mental consequences, one being the fashioning of a world, another being the location of a god and gods in that world. The latter is a consequence of the former: the mental rejection of a wider world is the psychic action which fashions the god.

Ultimately this limited world in which primitive man is confined has its drawbacks, even in terms of survival. Captive to a mentality which is inflexible it is unable to free the members of the tribe from the instinctual straitjacket in times of crisis. Confronted by a bad omen, the tribal member sacrifices a goat to his god. A scientist would plan a campaign as Joseph did when the Pharaoh had the dream of the seven fat cows followed by seven thin cows. Joseph responded to the dream with scientific forethought. If instead he had offered a goat to the god he would have been behaving with a primitive mind.

The violence done to the natural order in paring it down to the needs of the tribe causes the eruption of a god into the mythic world. The violent act by which the natural order is squeezed into the control of the communal psyche produces a vengeful retaliator: the god or gods, projected and made concrete in an animal, stream, mountain or the sun, who must be placated with sacrifices, rituals, invocations and ceremonies. This 'god' or these 'gods' is/are projected and made concrete in an animal, a stream, a mountain or the sun.

The first hominids of the Lower Pleistocene possessed a limited consciousness. The probability is that if they possessed language it was extremely limited. They did not bury their dead. When they did, it signalled a significant advance in mankind's level of consciousness; it was a Great Leap Forward. Whenever this occurred it brought with it positive fruits. (It is not certain when humans began to bury their dead. They were certainly doing so 60,000 years ago and they were not doing so 400,000 years ago. It is probably safe to place the beginnings of it about 100,000 years ago.) What is the difference between a society that tosses a body to one side to rot or be devoured by scavengers and one which pays respect to the dead body through religious ceremonial?

A ceremonial burial implies that the dead one has a life in the I-of-the-Other. The burial signifies that the individual who has died continues to live in the minds of the others as an 'I'. This realization articulates thought; it is the object of the thought. The transition from feeling to thought occurs at this point, as evidenced by my own observation of patients who have made this transition. I will give an example. A man was terrified of people in authority, as he felt such people were gods who would break him apart and shatter him. He aped me; he ingested my emotional approach to life; he existed *in* me. I did not exist as a person, but rather as a figure on a pedestal on a different plane from him. It became clear that he himself was included in this belief: the god on the pedestal was a merged reality of him-and-me in which there was no individual source of personal action. After five years of psychoanalysis an emotional upheaval occurred after which there were three significant changes: first, people in authority were no longer invested with god-like qualities: second, he saw me as a person who might experience pain and disappointment; and third, he began to have his own thoughts and the habit of ingesting my emotional attitudes greatly diminished. The psychological constitution of the tribe is constructed in the same way as this man's reality was before the change which occurred at the five-year mark. He lived a primitive religion: I was a god; his words were offered to placate me and he was merged with me. It was not even correct to speak of him as 'he' as there was no such entity until this emotional upheaval took place. In evolving man, psychological change of this kind also occurred and it is marked by man beginning to bury his dead. In my patient, the realization of a 'him' and a 'me' and the emergence of thought all occurred concurrently. 'I' is a concept. You do not feel 'I' – it is an object of thought. Feeling refers to surfaces, tactile stimulation on the skin and in the inner corridors of the body. What happened to my patient was the birth of the *representational self*. The mythology of a soul that lives on emerged at this time.

With the birth of the *representational self* comes awareness of illness, infertility, death, and consciousness reaches a new level. A being in its own right has died, not just a fragment of the tribe, or a limb of the body. With this awareness a new fear of inner dangers is aroused as the result of a knowledge of inner intentional action. Primitive man *knew* about the intentional power that one human being could wield over another; for example, a Dinka tribesman robbed of a beast by another may obtain for himself a *mathiang gok* (a fetish consisting of a bundle of roots) and invoke its power to speak to the conscience of the enemy, and threaten to injure him or his family. There is a link between injury or death and the intentional action of another. The power of intentional action is then feared in another; it is also feared in the self. There seems to be good evidence that illness or death can be brought about through the invocation of a fetish. In certain Aboriginal tribes in Australia it is asserted that death can be brought about through what is known as 'pointing the bone'.

That an individual experiences extreme guilt when he has defrauded his neighbour is a fact well attested in clinical practice. Extreme guilt is not felt but rather replaced by an experience of being hated by another. A man described his boss at work as narrow-minded, prejudiced and patronizing. His boss was like that and was a persecution to him. The man did not feel guilt, but he had instead the daily experience of his boss, whom he hated. Not even the persecution is felt when the guilt is extreme, just the hatred of the accusing finger that points. When a *mathiang gok* is invoked among the Dinka or a bone is pointed among the Aborigines the guilty individual is carved up inside emotionally, which frequently has a bodily effect. Profound guilt is incurred not only by such obvious actions as a man stealing another's beast, but also by the desire to do someone down. This desire, enacted even in the most subtle ways, brings about guilt, to which the anodyne word *anxiety* does not do justice.

Death then became attributable to intentional action. The Power, *Macardit*, in Dinkaland could cause the death of a man and so sacrifices are offered pleading *Macardit* to withdraw his influence. The world, this mythological envelope, becomes filled with intentional objects, the focus of whose activity is death. Death becomes experienced as an event caused by the threatening wishes of the possessor of *mathiang gok* but the Powers as well are thought to be material agents such as the *mathiang gok* but not identified with the material agents and are therefore spiritual powers bound to human agency, a spiritual power tethered to human desires through sacrifices and invocations. The offering of a sacrifice to the clan divinity *compels* that divinity into man's control, in the Dinka language. The term for such an offering is *mac*, which means 'tether' as when a beast is tethered to a peg.

When a man falls down dead through the threats issued by the Black Power, *Macardit*, or through the invocations of the one who possesses *mathiang gok*, the tribal group is able to assign meaning to the death: the death has occurred because the dead man has wronged someone. Death then is the wage of sin, as are sickness, infertility and economic misfortune. In the individual possessed of a *representational self* yet tied to the survival instinct death is the greatest punishment and as punishment it acquires meaning.

Primitive religion continues to exist in the bosom of all religious life today. Except in a few isolated pockets, such as among the Dinka, primitive religion does not exist as a pure culture, yet the mental attitude pervades all religions throughout the world. In mature religions there is always a tendency to regress to the mentality of primitive religion, a tendency which, as we shall see, has bedevilled religion throughout its long history.

Of the many complex upheavals that were occurring at the time of the Reformation one of the most fundamental was a violent protest against the belief that man, through a variety of superstitious practices, had God within his power. In the Christendom of the Middle Ages men, women and children believed they could purchase their salvation by kissing a relic, going on a pilgrimage or saying a ritualized series of prayers. It was against this magical system of beliefs that Luther and Calvin protested with such vigour.

The protest of Jesus was also against superstition rank at that time within Judaism. He protested against treating the Sabbath, the temple, and the festivals in a superstitious manner. The idea that by fulfilling all the prescriptions of the Law the worshipper found favour with God was condemned by Jesus in the most violent language. 'The Sabbath was made for man not man for the Sabbath' (Mark 2:27).

The Buddha also said that man does not find release from *dukkha*, suffering, through the rites and ceremonies prescribed by the Brahmins. Such sacrifices as practised by the Hindu priesthood would avail nothing. Release from suffering was found through right action.

However, the purity instigated by Jesus and the Buddha slowly degenerated so that both became stifled with precisely those superstitious practices whose influence they had lived and taught to combat. In the case of Buddhism later teachers claimed that the ideals of Buddhism were too high for ordinary folk who needed the psychological reassurance of superstitious practices. Mahayana Buddhism has fostered a cult of the Buddha himself and encouraged rites, sacrifices, and votive offerings, reaching its zenith in the Tantric Buddhism or Lamaism of Tibet. Theravada Buddhism has attempted to keep closer to the ideals of the historical Buddha.

Throughout the history of Christianity, pious men and women have arisen who have started new movements by paring away the current superstitions and reviving a purer form of Christian living. Before the Reformation there was St Bernard of Clairvaux, St Dominic and St Francis of Assisi. At the time of the Reformation and shortly after, there was St Teresa of Avila, St John of the Cross and St Ignatius of Loyola. Then after the Reformation within Catholicism such figures as St Thérèse of Lisieux and Père Foucauld and within Protestantism John Wesley and George Fox. It is, however, characteristic of all such movements that within a short period some of the superstitious superfluities banished by the founder of the school creep back, always justified with great barrages of rhetoric.

The truth of the matter is then that primitive religious mentality suffuses all the great organized religions of the world. In all these religious organizations there exists a tension between the pure doctrine of the founder and the accumulated layers of primitive elements that have slowly accreted to the organization as it has grown and developed. Primitive religion evolves from a primitive state of mind: the emergence of primitive religion, which we associate with the burial of the dead, represented a mental evolution, the emergence of a higher state of consciousness, where intentional action replaced pure instinctual action. However, individual action was still governed by the requirements of the survival instinct.

The cultic elements proper to primitive religion, to the extent to which they are present in the mind, prevent the development of conscience, which is the source of mature religion and healthy personality develop-ment. When we come to examine the psychological processes studied in psychoanalysis, we shall see the way in which such cultic elements betray a mental process that is antagonistic to the unfolding of mature religion.

There is a difference between primitive religion prior to the Axial Era and the regression to primitive religion from mature religion. In the latter there is a repudiation of higher knowledge; in the former this is lacking, altering the character of the mentality. Therefore it is necessary to make a distinction between a primitive religion which has not evolved to maturity and a primitive religious element which has come about through degene-ration. We shall use the term 'primitive religion' to indicate that religion that has not evolved to maturity, and 'primitive mentality' or 'primitive religious element' for that state of mind that has come about through degeneration.

REFERENCES

Henri Bergson (1935) *The Two Sources of Morality and Religion* (London: Macmillan & Co. Ltd), p. 123.
Godfrey Lienhardt (1987) *Divinity and Experience: The Religion of the Dinka* (Oxford: Clarendon Press).

2

Mature Religion

In what Karl Jaspers has identified as the Achsenzeit, *from very approximately 800 to very approximately 200 BC, significant human individuals appeared through whose insights – though always within the existing setting of their own culture – human awareness was immensely enlarged and developed, and a movement began from archaic religion to the religions of salvation or liberation.*

(Hick, 1989)

During the Axial Era (800–200 BC) there arose outstanding religious teachers who changed radically the religious outlook of mankind. Those who flourished included Confucius and Lao-tzu in China; the Buddha and Mahavira in India; Zarathustra in Persia; the Hebrew prophets Amos, Hosea, the Isaiahs, Jeremiah, Ezekiel; and Socrates, Plato and Aristotle in Greece.

While these people were the founders of the great religions which still hold sway today after two millennia, it would be a mistake to assume they have necessarily been the most spiritual. For instance, to the unprejudiced mind it would be difficult not to assert that Abu Hamid al-Ghazzali had reached greater spiritual depths than Muhammad. It seems probable also that mystics like St Francis of Assisi, Meister Eckhardt or St John of the Cross were more spiritual men than Jesus, the founder of the religion to which they belonged. I think it likely that the only religious founder who remained unsurpassed in spiritual achievement by his followers was Siddhartha, the Buddha.

Mature religion is characterized by certain elements which distinguish it radically from primitive religion. However, because there is usually a pre-history, elements of mature religion are frequently foreshadowed in the 'prophets' of primitive religion. For instance among the Dinka certain clansmen would be possessed by a free divinity and they were recognized by their clansmen as having special powers. Usually these powers were restricted within the cultic sphere; however, sometimes such a man would be recognized as having an understanding which went beyond this. For example Arianhdit was such a personality. It was said that his power was manifest not in hysterical possession, as was the case in many minor

14

divinities, but simply in the truth of his words. Arianhdit gained respect even outside the Dinka. Such a man is transitional between primitive and mature religion. It takes a further step to become a Jeremiah, a Buddha or a Socrates. The boundary between primitive and mature religion is not always clear-cut if it is remembered that primitive mentality continues to exist in mature religions just as primitive religions approximate towards mature religions. Because the boundary may be sometimes difficult to draw it does not mean that the two religious types are close in mental attitude.

The founders of mature religion held in common one element: they taught that it is useless to attempt to deal with the evil intentions of the heart by offering sacrifices or by partaking in ritual ceremonies. Instead they said it is necessary to *do* something, as it is by *doing* that man frees himself. And so we come to the central issue addressed by the teachers of mature religion: all offer a path, a way, a teaching that will grant freedom. The question is, freedom from what? There is a condition in which man finds himself, and from which he desires to be freed. We are given a clue about this condition if we return to the primitive religions and look at the reasons that lead primitive man to offer sacrifice. One reason, as we have seen, is that a strange omen appears that threatens the tribe's survival. The teachers of the mature religions however state quite simply that survival is *not* the ultimate goal; life has a deeper meaning, and the choice to die rather than to survive can be a meaningful alternative. The survival instinct drives men to avoid death, pain, illness and disease at all costs, but it has social consequences within the community that carry what may be termed a 'self-orientated' morality. The goal of the primitive mind is protection against illness, pain and death, which perhaps explains why some primitive minds seem inured to the injury inflicted on others. We might term such a person psychopathic, but we could also say they are operating within the confines of the primitive mind. It is a morality governed by the anxiety to please the one with power so as to ensure my own survival: those things that favour me and my tribe are pursued. This is referred to by religious people as a materialist philosophy. I must increase and add to those basic requirements for survival. For instance a nation's political strategy may based on the premise that economic growth is the prime goal, regardless of the consequences to other countries.

In the Dinka religion there is a myth of the Fall of Man as in the Judaeo-Christian mythology. I quote the myth as reported by Lienhardt:

A myth tells how Divinity (and the sky) and men (and the earth) were originally contiguous; the sky then lay just above the earth. They were

15

connected by a rope, stretched parallel to the earth and at the reach of a man's outstretched arm above it. By means of this rope men could clamber at will to Divinity. At this time there was no death. Divinity granted one grain of millet a day to the first man and woman, and this satisfied their needs. They were forbidden to grow or pound more. Divinity here clearly emerges as a person, with the attributes of father and creator, and conceptually distinct from the observable sky; in this context we can thus refer to Divinity with the personal pronoun, as 'he'.

The first human beings, usually called Garang and Abuk, living on earth had to take care when they were doing their little planting or pounding, lest a hoe or pestle should strike Divinity, but one day the woman 'because she was greedy' (in this context any Dinka would view her 'greed' indulgently) decided to plant (or pound) more than the permitted grain of millet. In order to do so she took one of the long-handled hoes (or pestles) which the Dinka now use. In raising this pole to pound or cultivate, she struck Divinity who withdrew, offended, to his present great distance from the earth, and sent a small blue bird (the colour of the sky) called *atoc* to sever the rope which had previously given men access to the sky and to him. Since that time the country has been 'spoilt', for men have to labour for the food they need, and are often hungry. They can no longer as before freely reach Divinity, and they suffer sickness and death, which thus accompany their abrupt separation from Divinity.

The Fall comes about through greed: the woman wanted more than the stipulated ration of a single millet seed a day. The materialist philosophy is sparked by greed and it is always antagonistic to the values of mature religion. Men's desires begin to supersede their survival requirements, which is an inevitable concomitant of the 'self-orientated' morality of the survival instinct. The reason for this is that man's desires are stimulated beyond need. So greed and other vicious habits of mind underpin the materialist philosophy of the primitive mind, which mature religions have all condemned.

It is a striking fact and an alarming one that as man's consciousness expands so also does his capacity to invest animal needs with narcissistic detritus. I will give a clinical example. I was once treating a woman who violently poisoned all developmental advance, pouring scorn upon all her best efforts. She also scorned all her animal needs and destroyed hunger by projecting recklessness into it, transforming it thereby into greed. In this way the survival instinct became infused with self-destructive reckless-ness. This is what I mean by the growth in consciousness having this bad

concomitant which is over and above the survival instinct. This reckless-
ness is a self-destruction. It goes contrary to the survival instinct. Freud
introduced the idea of the death instinct to explain this phenomenon.

It is a contradiction in terms to say that being driven by the survival
instinct is a meaning; meaning arises when there is choice, which has no
place when the subject is being driven. There is only social meaning when
the individual's activity is driven by the tribe's survival instinct. Meaning is
that human experience which arises when an individual is free to stand
against the dictates of drivenness. The early Christian martyrs were giving
witness (*marturion* in Greek means 'witness') to their belief that there was a
meaning to life which transcended death. This also is the principle of
religious ascesis, or self-discipline, the aim of which is to become detached
from the fear of not surviving.

Linked to the survival instinct is pleasure. There is pleasure in eating, in
defecating, in sexual intercourse. In traditional religion, ascesis has been
directed to detaching the individual from attachment to the survival
instinct via these pleasures; however, it is also clear from religious teaching
that detachment from these pleasures is not an end in itself. Meaning does
not lie in a negative. For example, after leaving his father's palace,
Siddhartha spent seven years with the ascetics in the Deer Park. He left
with the realization that the meaning of life is not to be found in the ascesis
itself, and shortly after achieved his supreme Enlightenment. He had first
to detach himself from his attachment to ascesis as a thing-in-itself.
Meaning cannot be grasped while the individual is attached to the
paraphernalia of the survival instinct as it lies above and beyond this. The
difficult question is: 'In what does the meaning consist?'

It is clear that these great religious teachers had discovered something
crucial to our understanding of life. Essentially this was not theoretical but
something that could only be understood in the living of it. It was
supremely practical. Although these teachers understood the meaning of
life, they were unable to express it in a logical, concise way. They could
point to it, tell stories, and give parables but the hearer had to grasp it
himself or herself. In the High Middle Ages, Thomas Aquinas, arguably
the most profound religious philosopher within Christendom, yet, at the
end of his life, had an intellectual vision which led him to exclaim that
everything which he had written was of straw. My attempt to locate where
meaning lies is bound therefore to be woefully inadequate.

Just before Enlightenment the Buddha had a supreme struggle with
Mara, the Evil One. In a similar way, Jesus had such a struggle with the
Devil, which is known in Christian mythology as the Temptation of Christ
in the Desert. Zarathustra also underwent such a struggle with the Evil

One in his initiation. When the seeker after truth detaches himself from the linkages of the survival instinct, he is then confronted with the spiritual realities of Good and Evil. Meaning lies in the choice; meaning is the choice; meaning is the choice of the Good. There is a profound difference between Good and Evil, though superficially they look similar. Evil has to look similar to Good in order to be chosen; only Good can be chosen, so Evil has to masquerade as Good in order to invite choice. In the person who chooses Evil we often recognize all the signs of detachment which we associate with the one who has chosen the Good. The greatest perpetrators of Evil have sometimes been relatively free of those material attachments which we associate with primitive religion; for instance, Hitler was abstemious in his eating and drinking habits, though he was sexually perverse.

We call religious leaders those who have in their spiritual struggle made the choice of the Good. Infamous leaders like Hitler and Stalin have chosen the path of destruction. However, even in such men, there are forces for good, but they become enslaved to Evil. What then are the characteristic notes of such a leader? Only the great figures in history have reached this level of ultimate choice as it can only be made subsequent to the detachment from 'worldly lusts', and most of us do not reach such a stage. It is probable, however, that the great sinners and the saints do. As for the great evildoer, I think it likely that though it appears he has achieved detachment from the 'lusts' of this world, the facts betray the opposite. In psychoanalytic language, the worldly attachment is split-off and channelled into a narrow funnel of perverse activity, usually in the sexual sphere, and there is an erotic attachment to power for its own sake.

The choice of the Good draws all the action spheres of the personality into a concentrated unity which endows the life of the individual with meaning and freedom. It bestows a freedom because it is never tied to a concrete reality: the Good is spiritual and never bound into one individual, organization, or piece of the world. Unlike Truth, it is not the object of intellectual assent, but of practical action. It cannot be made apart from Truth but the action engages the emotional life of the individual. Mystics, for example, combine contemplation and action in their lives. Contemplation follows the assent of Truth and is not separable from emotional action towards the Good.

Distinguishing between Good and Evil will help us to characterize the Good, and the instance of true and false mystics may give us the best lead. The false mystic plays to the gallery: the purpose of his piety is to bring praise and acclaim from those around or attachment to the charismatic power for its own sake. Mystics often wield such power but struggle to remain detached from it. The false mystic seeks power for its own sake. He is reinforced by emotional rewards coming from without and by sweet consolations from within. Attachment to visions and sweet delights in prayer are the goal of the false mystic. The inner act of knowledge is what sustains the true mystic and visions are distrusted; what sustains the false mystic is outer admiration and inner sensuality. Sensuality within can be as great as sensuality without; in fact I believe that it is much greater. We think of sensual gratifications in terms of delicate foods that delight the tastebuds and visual, auditory, tactile and sexual gratification. There is also an inner, sensual, unconscious imagery that gratifies the self. The puritanical individual who repudiates sensual pleasure but preens himself inwardly is motivating himself through gratification fuelled by inner images, as St Aelred of Rievaulx said: 'He who is proud of his chastity is vicious because pride is a vice.' This inner preening of the erotized self is hidden, or nearly hidden, to outward view. The most severe ascesis may inwardly be accompanied by intense inner grooming, itself accompanied by sensual imagery within, which holds the ego in thrall. There is an addiction to these sensually captivating images which power the direction of the individual's emotional life. In fact, the individual does all he can to bend the social environment to gratify them. The true mystic is detached from these inner images. Consequently he is not fixated on an incarnate external.

While it can be extremely difficult to distinguish between the true and false mystic, there are signs which over time betray the latter. The most noteworthy is an activity that is discrepant with the rest of the behaviour. For example Madame Acarie, who brought the Reformed Carmelite nuns from Spain and established them in France in the seventeenth century, received into the order a woman who displayed great piety. However, Madame Acarie began to distrust the sincerity of the woman's piety, suspecting her of reading her letters. One day, she put into an unsealed envelope containing a letter some minute pieces of paper, which would fall out if the letter was taken out of its envelope. Having laid this trap, she went out, and sure enough when she returned the tiny pieces of paper were no longer in the letter. In an ordinary person it would be a discredit to read another's letter, but in someone claiming such piety it reveals a false façade. Although it strikes one as obvious, it is worth investigating why this should be so. Psychoanalysts refer to such discrepant bits of behaviour as originating in a split-off part of the ego, holiness being consistent with integrated ego functioning. At its most obvious there are two pieces of behaviour that are at right angles to one another. The ego is split: from one part of the ego comes one piece of behaviour, and from another, another. It is possible that the individual may consciously not know about one set of behaviour when in the identity of the other. False mystics often shadow the true mystic, and in accounts of true mystics it is common to come across such imitators. A famous imitator was Brother Elias, the disciple of St Francis, who is responsible for building the resplendent tomb for the saint at Assisi. One of the most sumptuous tombs in all Italy is in dire contrast to the *poverello* whose bones it enshrines.

The true mystic makes a decision to be himself, while the false mystic slips into the identity of another. St Thérèse of Lisieux, at a particular moment in her adolescent development, was tempted to 'put on the cloak of sanctity' but managed to resist it (Görres, 1959). This notion of being another, especially when that other has acquired religious fame, is a keynote of the false mystic. The motivation is to acquire fame and have power as an end in itself. The end of the action is the inflation of the self, fuelled by a greed for power for its own sake which is the opposite to the intentions of a true mystic.

There are other signs that betray the disguises of the false mystic. For example the false mystic needs an external cloak in order to hide an inner state of disintegration which he cannot allow himself to know about. He shrinks from seeing himself, from knowing the ghastly deed done in the depths; his life is based on a basic refusal of personal life where instead the integrity of the ego and its objects has been smashed up.

What is the motivation of the true mystic? It is in and through *something* that man is freed. First he is freed from the fear of death, the constant threat of which hovers over him. Second, in that *something* life is invested with meaning through which he is freed from the constraints of the survival instinct, with the accompanying self-inflation. Offering a sacrifice to placate the god does not change the inner state of man. The teachers taught their followers to raise their hearts above the level of the survival motive. 'Greater love than this has no man', said Jesus, 'than he who lays down his life for his friends.' This is a sentiment central to the teaching of the mature religions. Life has a meaning which transcends the survival instinct, and is contrary to self-inflation.

In mature religion a person finds meaning in the direction or quality of his emotional activity towards himself and others. The object upon which he places value and in relation to which he acts transcends his own interests, his own desires for power or aggrandizement. A person is religious in this mature sense if this object has priority over all other concerns, and if in its service he detaches himself from inferior allurements.

Mature religion

The mental life of a person who has embraced the core values of mature religion is a world apart from someone dominated by the mentality of primitive religion. The failure of psychoanalytic writings to make this crucial distinction has led to much confusion.

REFERENCES

Aelred of Rievaulx (1942) *Christian Friendship* (London: The Catholic Book Club).
I. F. Görres (1959) *The Hidden Face: A Study of St Thérèse of Lisieux* (London: Burns & Oates).
John Hick (1989) *An Interpretation of Religion* (London: Macmillan Press), p. 29.
Godfrey Lienhardt (1987) *Divinity and Experience: The Religion of the Dinka* (Oxford: Clarendon Press), pp. 33–4.

3

The Judaeo-Christian Tradition

With what gift shall I come into Yahweh's presence
and bow down before God on high?
Shall I come with holocausts,
with calves one year old?
Will he be pleased with rams by the thousand,
with libations of oil in torrents?
Must I give my first-born for what I have done
wrong,
the fruit of my body for my own sin?
— What is good has been explained to you, man;
this is what Yahweh asks of you:
only this, to act justly,
to love tenderly
and to walk humbly with your God.

(Micah 6:6–8)

In your prayers do not babble as the pagans do, for they think that by using many words they
will make themselves heard. Do not be like them; your Father knows what you need before
you ask him.

(Matthew 6:7–8)

Our civilization is so permeated with the ideals of Judaism, Christianity
and Islam that it is extremely difficult to observe this tradition with an
outsider's detachment. The conflict between mature and primitive religion stands out most clearly in the entreaties of the prophets who had two
key messages: forsake the worship of false gods and return to Yahweh;
and righteousness is found not in sacrifices and religious ceremonies but
in behaving justly towards those whose predicament demands our
attention.

The great age of the prophets ran from the eighth to the sixth century
BC. In nearby Persia, Zarathustra also flourished at the same time with a
very similar message. He forbade the sacrifice of bovines and cursed the

22

worship of the *daevas*, the false gods of the pagans, and demanded the worship of *Ahura Mazda*, the Supreme Being.

The difference between Yahweh and the *baals* or false gods lay in representability. No image was to be made of Yahweh and as soon as Israelites represented him in visual form he had become a *baal*. Yahweh cannot be known through the senses: this is the clearest message of the prophets which is reiterated again and again in Israel's history.

The people find favour in the sight of Yahweh not by offering sacrifices but by good actions:

> What are your endless sacrifices to me?
> says Yahweh.
> I am sick of your holocausts of rams
> and the fat of calves.
> The blood of bulls revolts me . . .
> Take wrong-doing out of my sight.
> Cease to do evil.
> Learn to do good,
> search for justice,
> help the oppressed,
> be just to the orphan,
> plead for the widow.
> (Isaiah 1:14, 16–17)

Yahweh however is endowed with human attributes which are foreign, if not abhorrent, to the Hindu conception of Brahma. Brahma is ultimate reality and knowledge of it was arrived at through a process of asceticism, philosophical reflection on man's ontological composition and emotional enlightenment. In this tradition the reality which was thus apprehended was totally devoid of anthropomorphic qualities. This is quite untrue of the Judaic conception of Yahweh: although the prophets castigated the faithless people for building altars and statues, yet the very vehemence of their judgement gives us reason to suspect a projection, that Yahweh himself is endowed with sensory qualities. We do not have to go far to see the human qualities with which Yahweh has been endowed by the seers of the Israelites. Yahweh has made a special covenant with the Israelites over all the other peoples of the earth and this lies at the centre of Judaic religion. The fantasy that this tribe is preferred over all the other tribes is a remnant of primitive religion where my tribe's survival is paramount, although there were prophetical statements designed to counteract this, such as the famous one in Deuteronomy:

If Yahweh set his heart on you and chose you, it was not because you
outnumbered other peoples: you were the least of all peoples.

(Deuteronomy 7:7)

Yet the belief that Yahweh had chosen Israel and made this one tribe
special out of all the peoples of the earth remained unassailable. To the
extent to which this fantasy impregnated the conception of the Supreme
Being, exactly to that extent was Yahweh a false god, a *baal*. This primitive
mental quality passes on into Christianity and Islam and remains such
within the whole tradition to the present day. The belief that I am the
favoured one over all my siblings can only be maintained through a deep-
seated omnipotence.

The belief that salvation comes through performance of external ritual,
sacrifices and ceremonies is inextricably linked to worship of a false god.
The prophets railed against the belief that people could be liberated by
such procedures from the travails of human life but insisted instead that
they had to do good, search for justice and help the oppressed. What they
demanded was a transformation of heart but they were caught in a
dilemma which could not be solved because of their basic belief that
Yahweh had chosen Israel out of all the peoples of the earth. There is no
penetration through to an apprehension of reality like that achieved by
the seers of the Upanishads but it is masked instead by an image just as
sensory as the *baals* which the prophets condemned with such vehemence.
If you imagine one of the seers of the Upanishads cursing those who build
statues to false gods it makes no sense because they were themselves in a
different arena, unlike the prophets of ancient Israel. Believers in the
Judaeo-Christian tradition need to take to heart the words of Bede
Griffiths (1983):

In almost every country people of different religions and of no religion
are meeting with one another and being compelled to face their
differences. For a Christian and for members of the other Semitic
religions this presents a real problem. Each of them has been taught to
regard itself as the one true religion and to reject all other religions as
false, so that to enter into dialogue with other religions is not easy.

So, although the prophets were pushing for a mature religion, yet they
were still caught within a primitive mythology, and the attempts to solve
the human problems in our contemporary world within this ancient
tradition are doomed to failure unless there is a willingness to replace the

primitive mythology with a mature structure. This would mean abandoning Judaism, Christianity and Islam as we now know them but maintaining their core values.

What I have said of Judaism passed over into Christianity in the following way. Jesus, whose teaching was prophetical like his predecessors' of the earlier centuries, emphasized again that sacrifices and temple rituals were totally unable to free human beings from their psychological travails. This could only be found through following the demands of conscience:

> If you are bringing your offering to the altar and there remember that your brother has something against you, leave your offering there before the altar, go and be reconciled with your brother first and then come back and present your offering.
>
> (Matthew 5:23)

He spiritualized the Law:

> You have learned how it was said: *You must not commit adultery*. But I say this to you: if a man looks at a woman lustfully, he has already committed adultery with her in his heart.
>
> (Matthew 5:28)

> We ourselves have known and put our faith in God's love towards ourselves.
> God is love
> and anyone who lives in love lives in God
> and God lives in him.
>
> (1 John 4:15–16)

He condemned the idea that meaning could be found in outer rituals:

> Alas for you, scribes and Pharisees, you hypocrites! You who clean the outside of cup and dish and leave the inside full of extortion and intemperance. Blind Pharisee! Clean the inside of cup and dish first so that the outside may become clean as well.
>
> (Matthew 23:25)

Jesus' hatred of the scribes and Pharisees can be interpreted as a projection of a hated part of himself and this leads one to the reflection that he was partly responsible for bringing about the crucifixion.

He said his role was to bring the Law and the Prophets to fulfilment. So all the signs were that he had come to purify the Judaic religion of its primitive elements but we are met here with a bizarre contradiction: that his early followers erected him into a god so that his purification was replaced with a new idolatry even worse than that with which Yahweh had been endowed. Although in the early church the godhead which was in Christ Jesus was conceptualized in a spiritual way as existing in the hearts of believers, this later degenerated into a worship of the man Jesus himself as evidenced in the numerous statues throughout the world, but the Judaic exclusivity remained in a new form. Whereas Yahweh's chosen ones were the Jewish people, now it was all those who had been initiated into the Christian fellowship through baptism, and although in the early centuries of the church this implied an individual personal commitment of the heart, after the Peace of Constantine it became customary to incorporate a whole people into the church upon the conversion of the king of the territory, and today most people are baptized in infancy when the individual has no personal say in the matter. People are Christians by virtue of having been chosen by Yahweh in the same way as is true of members of the Jewish race.

The psychological components of this are the continuation of the false god with the accompanying ceremonies through which people believe they find salvation. The inner omnipotence is a necessary constituent of this belief and with it a passivity and deadening of inner psychic action. So the message of Jesus was a step forward in the process of outer to inner but then came a massive step backwards in the installation of Jesus as a new *baal*.

The split between Judaism and Christianity impoverishes both religions. Judaism has maintained its religion within the family and therefore its values are located in the relationships between people within that structure. From this point of view it is the religion which is closest to the thesis of this book: that the area where religion is required to exist by the structures of the contemporary world is in the emotional space between people. Freud, however, pointed out the hatred that frequently exists between people who are closely bonded together. It is here that the Jewish religion lacks something which has been kept more alive within the Christian tradition. Saints and mystics within Christianity and Islam are witnesses to the struggle which we all have between the forces of good and evil within our own souls. Such mystics have known the depths of evil of which humans are capable and their own achievements demonstrate a triumph in goodness of heroic proportions. This perspective is quite alien to the Judaic spirit and although it is possessed by Christian and Islamic

26

mystics it is always in isolation from close bonds and this is also so of Buddhist and Hindu mysticism. Jews need this vision of the Christian and Islamic mystics and Christians and Muslims need to place their insight within the emotional bonds existing between family members.

The primitive elements are even more manifest in Islam than in Judaism and Christianity. Although Muhammad has not been doctrinally divinized as Jesus has, yet unofficially he has. Within both these traditions the idealization of their founders has been extreme to the extent that within Islam criticism of Muhammad is a sacrilege that warrants the penalty of death. Allah, like Yahweh but more so, is endowed with human characteristics. Muhammad submitted himself to Allah and in ecstatic states he believed that he was transcribing Allah's doctrines and law as they were written on tablets in heaven into the words which now form the Koran, which has become an object of worship in itself. No textual criticism is permitted within Islam because the words of the Koran are sacred and not to be tampered with. We have here then worship characteristic of primitive religion. The mature religious elements are to be found within the Sufi mysticism and in some of the doctrines but they are locked away within a primitive framework.

All three traditions possess the core values of mature religion which has been passed on from generation to generation within them. However these core values, which endow interpersonal relations with meaning and are essential intrapsychically for the development of thought, are locked away within a primitive religious framework making them unavailable for use by secular men and women in our contemporary world.

REFERENCES

Philip S. Bernstein (1960) *What the Jews Believe* (London: W.H. Allen).
Paul Demann (1961) *The Jewish Faith* (Faith and Fact Books; London: Burns & Oates).
Mircea Eliade (1978) *A History of Religious Ideas* (University of Chicago Press), p. 304.
Erich Fromm (1972) *Psychoanalysis and Religion* (Bantam Books/Yale University Press).
Bede Griffiths (1983) *The Marriage of East and West* (London: Fount Paperbacks, HarperCollins), pp. 2–5.
Alfred Guillaume (1976) *Islam* (Harmondsworth: Pelican Books), p. 56.

4

Religious Wisdom From the East

At that moment, when the world around him melted away, when he stood alone like a star in the heavens, he was overwhelmed by a feeling of icy despair, but he was more firmly himself than ever. That was the last shudder of his awakening, the last pains of birth.

(Hesse, 1974)

It was in India during the Axial Era that spiritual wisdom reached its pinnacle in the Upanishads. There arose in the same Era in the Far East four giants of the spiritual life: Confucius, Lao-Tzu, Mahavira and the Buddha. We shall examine only the Upanishads and the teachings of the Buddha, as in them mature religion reached its highest expression.

Through intuitive wisdom the seers of the Upanishads pierced through the veil of sensuality to a knowledge of *atman*, a knowledge of the self which is at one with Brahma. The closest translation we can get to these two terms is the Self and Ultimate Reality respectively. This deep spirituality is embedded in the midst of a pantheon of gods, goddesses, rites, sacrifices and ceremonial of the most sensual kind. 'Hinduism' is a word coined by Europeans to refer to the religious practices of India and is therefore an umbrella word covering everything from the village cult of Ganesh to the Vedanta, the philosophy of the Upanishads. The outsider may feel lost in this disparate array but if its spiritual centre is grasped the rest falls into place with relative ease.

The Vedas, the earliest record of the Hindu religion, are poems glorifying the wonders of the external world. The passages that do hint at Brahma in the Rig-veda lack interiority. The Brahmanas which came at the end of the Vedic era are a compilation of rubrics and rites for sacrifices and mark a degeneration in religious practice. They typify a regression to primitive religion and the seers of the Upanishads arose in reaction to them. It seems that both in the individual and in culture the depths of degradation have to be plumbed before new life can arise. In the Israelite history a deeper spirituality arose after the Exile and so also in the

28

unfolding of religious consciousness in India. Many have considered that the deepest teaching about the mind, the psyche and the spirit is contained in the Upanishads and that they still remain unsurpassed. In the West the philosopher Schopenhauer was one of the first thinkers to recognize their pre-eminence.

Through our senses we perceive colour, sound, taste, smell, heat and cold. Philosophers have referred to these as the 'secondary qualities' of reality. Whereas we know this manifestation of reality through the senses we only know reality itself through an act of intuition. It is the diverse character of reality that is known through the senses, but its unity which is its essential nature is only known through insight. These Upanishadic seers were the first human beings to pierce through the *phenomenon* to the *noumenon*; this was the birth of abstract thought. The intentionality of human beings was born at the time when humans began to bury their dead and the second great evolutionary step in human consciousness was when these seers intuited Ultimate Reality from its sensuous encasement. These two phases in the development of human consciousness are permanently recorded in the phenomena of primitive and mature religion.

As there is nothing outside of Reality these seers realized that their own selves were part of it or, more accurately, were it: 'That thou Art' was then their deepest realization. This apprehension of their own existence was not an intellectual deduction such as that of Descartes two millennia later but a direct personal realization which can only be achieved through meditation and a personal detachment from the pull of the senses. It is this spiritual and mental detachment which differentiates religion from social welfare. Mystics have always believed and taught that the transformation of our human world cannot be achieved through social or political reform unless it is accompanied by this detachment of the spirit.

The process of detachment is not from sensual objects themselves but only in so far as they aggrandize the self. Ascesis can also aggrandize the self. William Law says,

> Hence we may learn the reason why many people not only lose the benefit, but are even the worse for all their mortifications. It is because they mistake the whole nature and worth of them. They practise them for their own sakes, as things good in themselves; they think them to be real parts of holiness, and so rest in them and look no further, but grow full of self-esteem and self-admiration for their own progress in them.
>
> (Huxley, 1980)

My own observation tells me that when an individual practises mortification for this motive he indulges unawares in unconscious sensual imagery; seeking, for instance, an admiration from others which captivates the unconscious imaginative processes. Ascesis which is genuine is a renunciation of the inflated self so that Atman can be realized. Reality, Brahma, just *is*. Self-inflation in all its guises disconnects the mind from Brahma, from the *is-ness* of his own being. Psychoanalysts refer to this inflated self as either *omnipotence* or *grandiosity* and some conclude that it is the source of mental illness. The apprehension of Atman has not been a psychoanalytic aim. The notable exception to this has been Wilfred Bion's conceptualization of 'O'. However, both the significance and the *praxis* recommended by Bion have only been followed by a handful of analysts.

Like the Buddha, the seers of the Upanishads were tolerant towards the ritual and ceremonial practices all around them. In this way they transcended the spiritual level achieved by Zarathustra, Jesus and Muhammad in the Near East and also Mahavira, the founder of the Jain religion in India. The capacity to tolerate those who practise a primitive religious mentality must be seen then as the very highest spiritual achievement and one which the people just mentioned did not manage. It is important to be receptive to the possibility that mystics and saints within Zoroastrianism, Christianity, Islam and Jainism may have surpassed the spiritual level of their founders.

Siddhartha Gotama, who lived in his father's palace in the greatest luxury, was entirely sheltered from any experience of illness, old age, death or voluntary ascesis. The legend says that at his birth his father had a premonition that he would leave home and become a recluse; so he established this protective regime. At about the age of sixteen Siddhartha married and had a son.

One day Siddhartha rode forth from the palace with Channa, his charioteer, and saw by the roadside a sick man; he asked what this was and was told that it was a man stricken with disease. Further on, Siddhartha saw an old man and again asked Channa what manner of man this was. The charioteer replied that it was a man in old age. Then they passed a body on the ground and Channa explained that this was the body of a man who had died. Finally, they passed a man with a shaven head and a tattered yellow robe. The future Buddha asked Channa what such an apparel signified and was told that it was the garb of a recluse. When Siddhartha returned to the palace, he thought deeply about what he had seen. In the quiet of the night he stole out of the palace and Channa took him to the edge of a forest, where he cut off his hair, took off his nobleman's clothes and donned the torn clothes of a beggar, and there Channa left him and Siddhartha set forth on his new life. He was aged twenty-nine and it occurred in about the year 534 BC.

For six years Siddhartha practised the most severe austerities together with a group of ascetics at the Deer Park in Benares but he came to realize that he would not achieve release from *dukkha*, or suffering, through an external practice alone. So shocked were the other ascetics when they saw him accepting a bowl of porridge from the Lady Sujata that they promptly left him. Until this point there was still something of the false mystic in Siddhartha but he now disengaged from this last vestige of attachment. So he sat cross-legged under a bodhi tree, determined that he would remain thus seated until he had attained Enlightenment. At this point, Mara, the personification of Evil, tried to dissuade him from his purpose and to overpower him, but now no evil, however powerful, could prevail against him. The Buddha came through this struggle victorious and, at the end of a long dark night, achieved Enlightenment. There is an obvious parallel here with the struggle Zarathustra had with Evil and also that of Jesus which is known at the Temptations in the Desert. It is significant that this only happened after the Buddha became detached from craving; only when the individual detaches himself from all such craving is he confronted with the full intensity of this spiritual struggle. This is the reason why detachment from craving is so much feared. The battle of the spirit that follows detachment from the senses is a dark terror of loneliness in which there is no consolation. The individual feels assaulted by an alien power which threatens to obliterate him. It is an experience of a fearful kind; a terror far worse than anything the material world can generate. Down through history the mystics have spoken of it.

What does Mara, this personification of Evil, tempt the spiritual person into? I believe it is basically to wreck himself, to throw away all he has gained. This is a power which takes possession of the inner man so he feels invaded by a satanic darkness where all his certainties are thrown into disarray. Everything becomes corroded with doubt and indecision. Perhaps the suggestions of this mocking power are right? At this moment of supreme crisis all that has been gained is at risk. It is possible that the Hitlers of history have inwardly submitted to such a power.

How this supreme event in the Buddha's life budded into a new religious movement incorporating the Sangha with an established doctrine need not detain us. It was the Buddha's own unique experience which became the source of his teachings of which the core are the Four Noble Truths.

The First Noble Truth is *dukkha*, which is usually rendered as 'suffering' in English but is a concept which is much wider and deeper than this; it embodies the idea of imperfection, impermanence, emptiness, insubstantiality but also the idea of happiness. *Dukkha* means the attachment to these qualities in so far as they are transitory and thereby block the apprehension of Ultimate Reality.

The Second Noble Truth is *samudaya*, which is how *dukkha* arises. It arises from a craving for sense pleasures and for knowledge, happiness, prestige and power. It is the craving for these that gives rise to *dukkha* and it is through this that we remain bound to existence.

The Third Noble Truth is *nirodha*, which means the cessation of *dukkha* is possible. The total cessation of *dukkha* is *nirvana*.

The Fourth Noble Truth is *magga*, which means the Path and constitutes what is called the Middle Way. The Buddha had learned that the search for happiness through the pleasures of the senses or through the practice of asceticism was a false trail because they are external. The Fourth Noble Truth emphasizes that the Path is in moral action and this is separated into eight categories known as the Eightfold Noble Path: right understanding, right thought, right speech, right action, right livelihood, right effort, right mindfulness and right concentration. These qualities combine compassion and wisdom. Buddhist psychology stresses the need for a development of both and that they need to complement each other. Meditation, whose purpose is to draw the mind from the pull of the phenomenal world and towards the contemplation of Ultimate Reality, is for the cultivation of right mindfulness and is central to Buddhist practice. It can be seen from this that Buddhism is a practical philosophy of the mind:

> It has nothing to do with belief, prayer, worship or ceremony. In that sense, it has nothing which may popularly be called 'religious'. It is a Path leading to the realization of Ultimate Reality, to complete freedom, happiness and peace through moral, spiritual and intellectual perfection.
>
> (Rahula, 1985)

Although we earthbound creatures cannot know the content and experience of the Buddha's Enlightenment yet, as it was *the* spiritual and psychological event of his life, we shall attempt to understand it. It cannot be a literal truth that Siddhartha had no contact with disease, old age and death in his father's palace; so what the legend signifies is that he was emotionally cut off from such realities. The ride with Channa represents the way he was shaken out of a trance-like state that had screened him from these aspects of reality. Until that time he had knowledge of these conditions but it was *inert* and did not grip his imagination or his desire to act. I refer to this kind of knowing as *inert knowledge*. In his awakening the knowledge of these realities became emotionally meaningful to him and stirred his imagination and fantasy life. I call his new state of mind one of *vital realization*. This transformation of *inert knowledge* into *vital realization* can be frequently observed in psychoanalysis and is one of its central aims. When a patient says, 'I have spoken about trust every day of my life but this is the first time I have truly understood what it means', it is an example of transformation from *inert knowledge* to *vital realization*.

The Buddha now started on the path which was to obliterate suffering. He knew that the root of suffering lies in a thirst or craving. (The word *tanha* translates better as 'craving' or 'thirst' than 'desire'.) Behind all craving, be it sensual, sexual, mental or spiritual, is the wish to inflate the self. He set about relinquishing this craving along with the other ascetics in the Deer Park. We may conjecture that he realized that the austerities had become objects of desire in themselves. Very frequently someone is addicted to extreme austerities out of guilt. If this is the case then we can suppose that his departure from the Deer Park represented a dissolution of guilt. All psychic activity now emanated from the ego rather than the super-ego.

Karma, the belief that mankind fashions his own destiny, lies at the centre of Buddhist doctrine: that which he sows is that which he reaps. If he does not reap it in this life than he reaps it in a subsequent life. This is in stark contrast to the Judaeo-Christian belief that God may rescue man from his sins and from the consequences of his own actions. The doctrine of *anatta* in Theravada Buddhism explicitly denies the existence of God. The meaning of the human condition and not salvation from it is the aim of Buddhism. This is well illustrated by comparing the following two events; one from the life of Jesus and the other from the life of the Buddha:

When he was near the gate of the town it happened that a dead man was being carried out for burial, the only son of his mother, and she was a widow. And a considerable number of the townspeople were with her. When the Lord saw her he felt sorry for her, 'Do not cry' he said. Then he went up and put his hand on the bier and the bearers stood still, and he said, 'Young man, I tell you to get up.' And the dead man sat up and began to talk, and Jesus gave him to his mother. Everyone was filled with awe and praised God saying, 'A great prophet has appeared among us; God has visited his people.'

(Luke 7:12–17)

Kisa Gotami lost her only child and became almost mad with grief, not allowing anyone to take away her dead child in the hope that it might revive again through some miracle. She wandered everywhere and at last came into the presence of the Buddha. Buddha understood the deep sorrow that so blinded the poor mother, so after giving her comfort he told her that he could revive the child if she could procure a handful of mustard seeds from the house of one where no death had ever taken place. Hope came to her and she set forth from house to house asking for a handful of mustard seeds. She did receive, everywhere, the seeds with profuse sympathy. But when it came to asking whether there had been any death in the family, everybody universally lamented the loss of a mother or a father or a son or daughter, and so on. She spent hours travelling in search of the precious seeds that promised the revival of her son, but alas, none could give them to her. A vision arose before her and she understood the implication of the Buddha's hint. She understood that death is inherent in life which is the source of all suffering, all delusion. To overcome life and death is to attain the highest security and freedom from suffering, which is the true significance of the holy life. With the dawn of this insight she felt a great relief, whereupon after having performed the last rites for her child she went to the Buddha and asked for admission into his Order of Nuns.

Reincarnation is necessary in order to uphold the logic of the doctrine. If a man is born blind, then it is because he has sinned in a previous life. The crucial question is, however, 'By what sort of action does a man or woman find release from suffering?' The Buddha is clear that it is not through any accident of birth, or through the performance of ritual or sacrificial offerings, or through performing austerities. A person does not find *nirvana* through knowledge as taught in the Upanishads but through moral action, and the individual has to grasp what this is in a free act of understanding.

The Buddhism I have been describing is the doctrine as taught by the Theravada School, sometimes known as Hinayana or Buddhism of the Southern School. In the third century after the Buddha's death many converts to Buddhism were political rather than spiritual and many of these swung back to Brahmanism:

> The negative philosophy of the Hinayana could never easily become a popular religion. When Buddhism became universal in spirit and embraced large masses, the Hinayana could no longer serve. A religion more catholic, a less ascetic ideal, was required.
>
> (Humphreys, 1955)

Under Mahayana and even more in Tantric Buddhism the Buddha was deified and within Hinduism was believed to be the ninth incarnation of the Lord Krishna. Salvation was by faith rather than meritorious acts. This deification of the Buddha combined with superstitious rites was the most baneful aspect of this degeneration; on the other hand the erection of a metaphysical system was helpful because practical wisdom needs a metaphysical foundation.

The Buddha himself said the path was through right mindfulness and the other qualities enumerated in the Eightfold Noble Path and not through the performance of Brahmanic rites and ceremonies. He believed this deeply and taught it with emphasis. However he taught his followers to respect Brahmanism. This attitude is quite different to that of Jesus towards the scribes and Pharisees.

I believe that Buddhism has a religious philosophy close to the value system of psychoanalysis. However it is a traditional religion and suffers thereby from limitations for the emotional life of man in the modern world. Its spiritual path is that of *fuga mundi*. The Buddha left his wife and son and found Enlightenment in isolation, alienated from close intimacy. For this reason Buddhism, like other traditional religions, fails to meet modern man in the emotional locus where he lives.

REFERENCES

Edmund Capon (1993) Taped commentary on 'Imperial China' Exhibition (New South Wales Art Gallery).

Erich Fromm (1972) *Psychoanalysis and Religion* (United States and Canada: Bantam Books), p. 16.

Bede Griffiths (1983) *The Marriage of East and West* (London: Fount Paperbacks, HarperCollins).

Hermann Hesse (1974) *Siddhartha* (London: Picador), p. 33.

Christmas Humphreys (1955) *Buddhism* (Harmondsworth: Pelican Books), p. 48.

Emotion and spirit

Aldous Huxley (1980) *The Perennial Philosophy* (London: Chatto and Windus), p. 124.

Lao-Tzu (1987) *Tao-Te Ching* (Harmondsworth: Pelican Books).

Walpola Rahula (1985) *What the Buddha Taught* (London and Bedford: Gordon Fraser), pp. 49–50.

5

Socrates – Religious Teacher in Classical Greece

The founder of every new religion possessed at first no greater authority than the founder of a new school of philosophy. Many of them were scorned, persecuted, and even put to death, and their last appeal was always, what it ought to be – an appeal to the spirit of truth with us, and not to twelve legions of angels, nor, as in later times, to the decrees of Councils, to Papal Bulls, or to the written letter of a sacred book.

(Max Müller, 1985)

Socrates was one of the great religious teachers of the Axial Era, although he is not usually recognized as such because he did not found a religious dynasty, or at least he is the only such teacher who remains well known to posterity.

The Socrates I refer to is the one we meet in the dialogues of Plato. Most scholars are agreed that in the *Republic* and the *Laws* the Socrates we meet is merely Plato's puppet, mustered to portray Plato's philosophical arguments and probably somewhat distant from the historical Socrates. The man we are studying here is the Socrates of the early dialogues, which are much more faithful to the historical Socrates as he was.

In a manner similar to the Buddha and Jesus, Socrates challenged the primitive religion current in Greece at the time. He preached a morality as elevated as that of the Buddha and Jesus, teaching how people should live and outlining the principles on which his morality was based. His principles bear all the marks of a morality which characterizes a mature religion, transcending the ordinances that are governed by the survival instinct. The religion of Socrates differs from that of the Buddha and Jesus in that it resulted from a process of reasoning.

It is perhaps clearer in Socrates's teaching than in any other that the doctrine being proposed is for the benefit of man, but because his principles were not incorporated in a living community of faith and

37

organized for posterity it is more accurate to call the doctrine of Socrates a spirituality rather than a religion.

The epitomy of his spiritual teaching is contained in the *Gorgias*. The dialogue consists of three arguments which Socrates has with the three Sophists: Gorgias, Polus and Callicles. Gorgias, an elderly man, is a famous professor of oratory with a considerable reputation. At that time in Athens, oratory was an extremely important skill; a man's life could depend upon it as the most important issues of the day were settled by public debate within the citizen body. Gorgias says that oratory consists in:

> The ability to convince by means of speech a jury in a court of justice, members of the Council in their Chamber, voters at a meeting of the Assembly, and any other gathering of citizens whatever it may be.

Having drawn this truth out of Gorgias, Socrates shows that the art of oratory is not concerned with ethical matters:

> The orator does not teach juries and other bodies about right and wrong – he merely persuades them . . .

One learns that Socrates is concerned to teach what is right and wrong. The orators however are not concerned with this, but only to persuade a jury to the view of the tyrant. Socrates challenges the prevailing assumption of the Sophists that might is right. At the end of his debate Socrates draws the conclusion that the orator has the knack of convincing his audience, and it is in this that the skill of his trade consists.

In the dialogue with Polus, Socrates goes on to say more directly that oratory is not an art but 'a sort of knack gained by experience'.

POLUS: A knack of doing what?
SOCRATES: Producing a kind of gratification and pleasure.

Socrates then goes on to say that oratory is a kind of pandering:

> Pandering pays no regard to the welfare of its object, but catches fools with the bait of ephemeral pleasure and tricks them into holding it in the highest esteem.

A bit later Socrates says,

> Now I call this sort of thing pandering and I declare that it is dishonourable – I am speaking to you now, Polus – because it makes pleasure its aim instead of good, and I maintain that it is merely a knack and not an art because it has no rational account to give of the nature of the various things which it offers.

Just before this Socrates has said that there is such a thing as:

> . . . an unreal appearance of health. For example many people appear to enjoy health in whom nobody but a doctor or trainer could detect the reverse . . . I maintain that there is a condition of soul as well as body which gives the appearance of health without the reality.

A remarkable insight into the fact that an apparently healthy façade may conceal an unhealthy soul. Socrates's teaching about the false self antedates Winnicott by 2,400 years. He also has a clear doctrine of the true self:

> Better that the mass of mankind should disagree with me and contradict me than that I, a single individual, should be out of harmony with myself and contradict myself.

We come here to one of Socrates's central doctrines: that man's end is the good and not pleasure. It is this that raises him above the mentality of primitive religion. It also raises him above the academic philosopher into the ranks of sainthood because he not only teaches an elevated doctrine but at the same time lives what he teaches, putting his principles higher than his own life.

For Socrates then the good is the end of man. To value a man is to know what is good for him. Towards the end of the dialogue he says,

> This conclusion alone stands firm, that one should avoid doing wrong with more care than being wronged, and that the supreme object of a man's efforts, in public and in private life, must be the reality rather than the appearance of goodness.

However, Socrates does not tell us what the good is and this question confronts us: what is the relationship between the good and pleasure? The answer I believe must lie in the distinction between the ephemeral and the eternal, which links with the distinction made earlier between primitive and mature religion. Pleasure is tied to physical survival and Socrates says we must aim to transcend this and reach the good. On the criterion we have adopted for distinguishing between primitive and mature religion, this makes Socrates one of the great spiritual leaders of mankind.

Does it mean, however, that to pursue the good robs the individual of pleasure?

> . . . happiness is not to be found in having a good time . . . it consists rather in doing something which appears to you to be worthwhile, and then looking back and noticing you have been happy.
>
> (Ashby, 1968)

Freud moves in this direction when he suggests that immediate gratification must be sacrificed in favour of delayed gratification. Freud, however, is tied to a survival theory and is therefore unable to make the distinction between the good and pleasure as Socrates has done.

It appears crucial to know of what the good consists, and it is here that Socrates fails us, or does he? While he does not provide a concrete answer, yet he does give us some signals which will lead us to the good, if we are careful to follow them.

This is one of the common denominators of all great spiritual teachers. The good as a spiritual quality must be grasped through a realization of the inner eye. It is never possible for a teacher to say '*This* is the good'. This is because the good lies not in any one object but between objects:

> *Between* the subject and the object lies the value. This value is more immediate, more directly sensed than any 'self' or any 'object' to which it might be later assigned.
>
> (Pirsig, 1991)

When Jesus was asked, 'And who is my neighbour?' he told a story the moral of which is obvious, yet it has to be told in that way because the answer to the question cannot be placed in an object or in the subject: it is *between*.

The good is something definite and realizable but yet not concretely locatable. It is a real object that can only be grasped through psychic action. In this way it is like truth, but it differs from truth in that the action demanded requires not only intellectual assent but emotional action. The difference between these two is enormous and we shall return to it.

The Buddha and Jesus both point us in the direction of the good.
Socrates also gives us signs, for example, in the dialogue with Polus:

s: . . . the greatest of all misfortunes is to do wrong.
p: But surely it is worse to suffer wrong?
s: Certainly not.
p: Do you mean to say that you would rather suffer wrong than do
     wrong?
s: I would rather avoid both; but if I had to choose one or the other I
     would rather suffer wrong than do wrong.

This reply of Socrates is very important. He would not choose to suffer
wrong; he is not a masochist. Like Thomas More, he would use all his skill
to defend himself.

Socrates also condemns the praise of power. He means the sort of
power a dictator wields or which an orator wields in the service of a
dictator. Power is a means to an end and only deserves praise if it is being
used in the service of the good.

Of two wrongdoers, Socrates says the happier is the one who is
punished. Punishment may cure the wrongdoer of his evil ways; he arrives
at this by logical deduction, through a process of reasoning. As medicine
heals the body, so punishment corrects the mind of the wrongdoer. Doing
harm is a greater evil than suffering pain. Justice is the 'moral physician'
that cures a man of wickedness, therefore the man who is punished is
happier.

In the dialogue with Callicles Socrates says that the good is the object of
all actions and that all we do is a means to the good: ' . . . we should
embrace pleasure among other things as a means to good, and not good as
a means to pleasure'. We get some insight into Socrates's conception of the
good.

Another important feature of Socrates's teaching is that his religious
message is addressed to those living in the hurly-burly of daily political life.
He does not invite the individual to leave the marketplace of his life; he
does not say that those who really want to follow the good path must leave
their everyday preoccupations to do so. In fact he points to the good and
not to himself. He differs from Jesus, who tells his disciples to follow
himself. He is also unlike the Buddha as he did not set up an institution as
the Buddha did.

What Socrates taught implied that the worship of the gods who
sanctioned the political ideologies of Athenian life should be renounced.
Although he was not vituperative towards the worshippers of the gods in

41

the way Jesus was towards the scribes and Pharisees, yet he did not have the Buddha's tolerance. It was for this reason that he was ultimately put to death by the Athenian courts.

By careful argument Socrates establishes that the good can neither be identified with pleasure nor evil with pain. This is in stark contrast to Freud, who does make exactly that identification. Whereas Freud says that a pleasure may have to be renounced in favour of delayed gratification Socrates says that the renunciation is in favour of a good that belongs to a different category. This good is known through conscience and in an act of judgement whereas suffering wrong is experienced in the feelings. Someone who believes in the doctrine of hedonism is compelled to argue that suffering wrong rather than doing wrong is the greater evil.

Although feelings are judgements, the implication of Socrates's teaching is that they are only reliable as guides to action if they are underpinned by an inner commitment to the higher principle of the good. Feelings will tell you when you are suffering wrong. If someone hits my hand with a stick I feel pain but not when I hit someone else with a stick. Is there any interior signal that would tell me not to hit another with a stick? Yes, conscience. What if I derive great pleasure from hitting someone with a stick? Is there any reason why I might obey my conscience which signals me not to hit my friend with a stick? If the seeking of pleasure or the avoidance of pain are my only guides, there is no reason for me not to – after all it gives me great pleasure.

Socrates then was one of the spiritual giants of the world's history but has largely gone unrecognized as such because he did not found a religious organization. He is thought of as a philosopher, perhaps even as a moral philosopher, but not as a spiritual man. He is not compared with the Buddha or Jesus, yet I believe he is a better model for the contemporary world than either of these because he established a spirituality based on reason, which is accessible to the thinking person. It is a rational spirituality concerned with how people are to live a virtuous life in the world. Unlike the Buddha or Jesus, Socrates taught a spirituality to be lived in the world. There was no command to separate from the human commonwealth; it was a spirituality devoid of ritual, that sought humility, wisdom and the acquisition of virtue. It was a teaching that was accessible to the person bustling his way through the forum and to modern man in his love affairs, in his business practice, in his leisure.

Socrates is a teacher of natural religion, meaning that it is accessible to reason and does not have to have recourse to any form of revelation. Whether Socrates had any experience of Enlightenment is not recorded; that he went into trances that lasted for a whole day and during which he

seemed to be engaged in concentrated thought is recorded, but the tag
that Freud so rightly deplored – *credo quia absurdum* – is equally deplored
by a Socratic spirituality. John Macmurray, the moral philosopher, has
explored the rational roots of natural religion and I shall try to summarize
his view, which I believe is the natural outcome of a religious quest in
contemporary times and one that is available to those capable of detaching
themselves from the seductive pull of either traditional religion or a
positive philosophy. The natural religion of John Macmurray is a Socratic
religion in the context of our contemporary world.

The field of science, aesthetics and religion, says Macmurray, is that of
common human experience. What differentiates the three is the attitude
of mind which is brought to that common field: the scientific attitude
studies and judges the world in terms of its utility to man; the aesthetic
attitude is one in which things are enjoyed and admired for their intrinsic
beauty. In each of these, the objects of the world are for our use or for the
gratification of our higher sensibilities; the objects are our servants, if not
our slaves. In the religious attitude there is acknowledgement that the
human world has a claim upon us because each of us has a value which
demands recognition. Macmurray (1936) says,

> The primary fact is that part of the world of common experience for
> each of us is the rest of us. We are forced to value one another, and the
> valuation is reciprocal.

The recognition that the 'other' has a claim on me is the religious attitude
of mind, and the inner signal of this claim is conscience. If I derive
pleasure from hitting another with a stick there is no principle within the
aesthetic which commands me not to. It is the religious attitude of mind
that attempts to deter me. Socrates said this claim is exerted upon me by
the good. Macmurray puts this into a modern perspective by stating that
the good is in the other, or that the good is immanent in other human
beings, and that this has a claim upon my actions.

Macmurray puts forward the view that God symbolizes this claim that
the other has upon me. This point is paralleled by Erich Fromm who says
that 'God is a symbol of *man's own powers*'. I believe however that
Macmurray has defined the symbolic referent more accurately than
Fromm. Defining God as a symbol of man's own powers says nothing
about how those powers are used. Macmurray says that the symbolic
referent lies in the 'other'. I should like to add to Macmurray that this
'other' should not be equated with the separate human being whom I see
'out there', but rather with the Ultimate Reality as comprehended in the

Upanishads, which is in me as well as in the other. Macmurray emphasizes that this Reality exists within the human community and is inseparable from it. What Socrates named the good is equivalent to the Ultimate Reality of the Upanishads.

Macmurray defines the religious sphere in this way:

> The religious attitude sets the relationship of the self to other selves at the centre of valuation and values everything else in relation to this. For such an attitude the main business of life consists in understanding, appreciating, and creating the full reality of personal relationship. The task of religion is the realization of fellowship. The religious activity of the self is its effort to enter into communion with the Other.

The work of creating the full reality of a personal relationship is the religious task. The field of religion is the human community, and it is within it that its work is to be done. It is a false trail to go outside of it.

The field of psychoanalysis is also within the human community as it is concerned with that emotional activity of which we are unaware. It is concerned with activity that occurs between people, which we do not know about, and, even more, with that which occurs within the frontiers of the self, of which we are also unaware. This unseen activity is 'emotional interaction', consisting in interpersonal interaction and intrapsychic interaction, and is the proper study of psychoanalysis. However patients come for psychoanalysis not to be guinea pigs in the psychoanalyst's laboratory but because they want to be healed of their ills. It is an aim, therefore, of psychoanalysis to transform activity which is invisible and destructive into that which is constructive but in a sphere which was not known by the Hebrew prophets, by Jesus, by the seers of the Upanishads, the Buddha or Socrates. It is this sphere then to which we now turn.

REFERENCES

Roy Ashby (1968) *Where Shall I Sow My Seed* (Doddington: The Stansfield Association), p. 7.

Walter Hamilton (1960) Introduction to Plato's *Gorgias* (Harmondsworth: Penguin Classics), p. 15.

John Macmurray (1936) *The Structure of Religious Experience* (London: Faber & Faber), p. 28.

— (1957) *The Self as Agent* (London: Faber & Faber).
— (1991) *Persons in Relation* (Humanities Press).
F. Max Müller (1985) *The Vedanta Philosophy* (New Delhi: Cosmo Publications), pp. 12–13.
R. M. Pirsig (1992) *Lila – An Inquiry into Morals* (London: Corgi Books), p. 84.

6

The Relation Between the Moral and the Spiritual

Now I would say that the experience of choosing imparts to a man's nature a solemnity, a quiet dignity, which never is entirely lost. There are many who set great store upon having seen one or another distinguished world-historical personality face to face. This impression they never forget, it has given to their souls an ideal picture which ennobles their nature; and yet such an instant, however significant, is nothing in comparison with the instant of choice. So when all has become still around one, as solemn as a starlit night, when the soul is alone in the whole world, then there appears before one, not a distinguished man, but the eternal Power itself. The heavens part, as it were, and I chooses itself – or rather, receives itself. Then has the soul beheld the loftiest sight that mortal eye can see and which never can be forgotten, then the personality receives the accolade of knighthood which ennobles it for an eternity. He does not become another man than he was before, but he becomes himself, consciousness is unified, and he is himself. As an heir, even though he were heir to the treasure of all the world, nevertheless does not possess his property before he has come of age, so even the richest personality is nothing before he has chosen himself, and on the other hand even what one might call the poorest personality is everything when he has chosen himself; for the great thing is not to be this or that but to be oneself, and this everyone can be if he wills it.

(Kierkegaard, 1972)

We have seen that a crucial difference between primitive and mature religion is that the activity demanded of the individual by the latter is 'circumcision of the heart': an attitude of compassion towards our fellow human beings. Morality is our mental intent towards our neighbour and towards our own selfhood. True spirituality incorporates the moral.

Self-centredness means that my neighbour is a slave to my needs. If I am successful in this endeavour, it would seem logically to mean that I shall be emotionally satisfied, but this is not so. There are two modes of action possible to the self. One is where I use others as objects to inflate my own self; the other is where I give emotionally towards others with no reward in view. The latter, though not intended, leads to an enrichment of the self whereas the former leads to its impoverishment. Therefore action either enriches or damages the self. Action that damages the self is immoral and

46

action that enriches it is moral. Shyness, feelings of inferiority, lack of confidence and so on are associated with immoral action.

True spirituality consists in directing psychic attention to the job of purifying moral action. Detachment is necessary in order to isolate the mental act and to determine its source and its object. It is not possible to purify the mental act without this detachment. Mystics and spiritual writers of all religious traditions stress the likelihood of self-deception; the tendency to believe in our righteousness is deeply rooted. Therefore, a central spiritual endeavour is to achieve knowledge of our own motivation. The purer the motivation the better is the behaviour that flows from it.

Purifying motivation means changing bit by bit the nature of our acts. It means that knowledge leads to an alteration of action, so action is the goal. The purer the action, the greater the knowledge of what is impure. Those who are high on the spiritual path see clearly their diminishments. Knowledge encourages action and action leads to new knowledge. St Augustine put it that knowledge leads to the act of love and love opens the door of knowledge.

Spirituality is that mental discipline whose goal is the purification of motivation. The focus of psychoanalysis is upon our motivation, but it does not rest there. Patients who come for psychoanalysis do so because they are suffering mentally. They therefore want to do something about their condition. They are not just observers of their motivation, but they also seek to purify it. Our unavoidable conclusion is that psychoanalysis has a spiritual function.

The spiritual person is one for whom this task of purifying motivation has become the organizing centre of his activities. Moral development through the course of a person's life is only possible through the stewardship of a dedicated spirituality. Spirituality is essentially individual whereas religion is the institutionalization of the spiritual enlightenment of the individual.

The aim of false spirituality, like false mysticism, is the enhancement of self-inflation. It aims to give the self the *feeling* of righteousness without having to act morally. False spirituality bypasses morality. The types of spirituality which have shown themselves to be false in this way are the gnosticism which was prevalent in the early centuries of the Christian era, the Jansenism which arose in France in the seventeenth century, and those modern spiritualities which depend upon drugs for their activation. What typifies all these spiritualities is their divorce from moral action. Frequently these spiritualities are compatible with degrading sexual orgies and activities which are damaging to the self and others.

Emotion and spirit

That we are moral beings means that our lives are the products of the choices we make. These are frequently made by a part of ourselves that we are not aware of. Spirituality is simply the attention which we give to these choices that are enacted at every moment of our lives.

True spirituality is attention to the moral dimension in our lives. It is false thinking then to separate morality from spirituality: there can be no moral development without a spirituality to sustain it and deepen it, and a spirituality divorced from morality only fosters the illusion of righteousness.

REFERENCE

S. Kierkegaard (1972) *Either/Or* (Princeton, NJ: Princeton University Press), vol. 2, p. 181.

7

Towards a Definition of Religion

Religion is the opium of the people.
(Karl Marx)

Primitive religion began at that point when humans started to bury their dead and mature religion began with those great spiritual masters who arose in the Axial Era. These are two phylogenetic milestones in the history of human consciousness. We are equating religion, then, with consciousness of selfhood.

What had humans become conscious of that led them to bury their dead? The burial of the dead was a sign of an inner change and realization. Until then, a member of the tribe was just a unit in an organization – there was no autonomous determining part. Using the analogy of the body for the tribal group, the individual member was equivalent to a limb. Guy de Maupassant has a short story where a sailor loses an arm in a naval accident and they bring the arm to shore and give it a burial. This gives the reader a weird feeling: we do not bury an arm because it has no selfhood. In a similar way, at an early stage in hominization the human tribe did not bury an individual member.

The first archaeological evidence for ritual burial coincides with the emergence of Neanderthal Man – *Homo sapiens neanderthalensis*. The fossil record indicates that Neanderthal Man appeared about 100,000 years ago and became extinct about 40,000 years ago. He lived through the last Ice Age, which began 70,000 years ago. He developed most probably from *Homo erectus* and his extinction coincided with the evolution of modern man – *Homo sapiens sapiens*. What is certain is that the Neanderthals buried their dead whereas *Homo erectus* did not. There is one particularly striking find from the Shanidar cave of the Zagros Mountains in Iraq. The body of a man was buried here 60,000 years ago and the skeleton is surrounded by dense clusters of pollen which could only have come from whole flowers which were not random but had been carefully arranged. Richard Leakey

49

interprets this as clear evidence for the fact that Neanderthal Man had a deep feeling for the spiritual quality of life. This is in accordance with his desire to prove that ancient man was altruistic in his inherent nature. It is, I believe, stretching the evidence to claim that Neanderthal Man was altruistic on that evidence but to bury the dead with such attention denotes respect and this means a recognition of selfhood. This means that the individual's activity had an intentional source. Therefore Neanderthal Man had evolved a selfhood and with this began what we classify as primitive religion.

What is meant by selfhood? To answer this question we have to look at the tribal group and compare it with a group of apes. The gorilla group, for instance, has a social organization necessary for its survival. The human tribal group also has an organization necessary for its survival. In the latter the means of ensuring that the individual members toe the line is through the threat of psychological punishment. In the gorilla group the threat is of a direct physical kind. The silverback who is the leader of the group threatens any deviance with physical punishment. In the tribal group the deviant one is punished at least with psychological isolation.

Among the Pygmies of the Ituri Forest in Zaïre where there is no hierarchical organization of society the group punishes deviance by isolating the culprit. In Colin Turnbull's book *The People of the Forest* where he lived with the Pygmies for at least two years, he describes how Cephu cheated the others on a hunting expedition. The Pygmies hunt by spreading out nets among the trees of the forest and then the women and children function as beaters and animals rush into the net. It is a venture which depends upon group co-operation. Cephu had secretly gone ahead and put out a net some distance ahead of the communal net and caught an animal and took it home, but was found out. This kind of individual acquisitiveness that sabotages the group effort is one of the most serious of crimes among the Pygmies. Cephu was therefore banished for some hours from social intercourse with the rest of the group. Although this may not seem much of a sanction Turnbull says that in a society where social togetherness is the very essence of their lives it is a very severe punishment.

There is already in the ape group some element of psychological threat but lower down the evolutionary scale it is much less. There are thus two different modes of ensuring the individual's obeisance: instinct and religion. In the instinctual mode the herd or the group has an acting principle in which all members participate and have no option to do otherwise. This was also the situation in the human group until humans started to bury their dead.

You honour someone when you realize that the contribution to the group was a matter of the individual's choice, so the ultimate scorn of an individual is to refuse him or her burial. For example in Sophocles's play *Antigone*, Antigone determines to go against Creon's injunction that Polyneices be not buried but left on the field of battle for the birds of carrion to devour. Honouring the dead with burial is a sign that the individual has made a contribution which the group is required to honour. We shall call this evolutionary step when humans began to bury their dead the *burial climax*.

The realization that the individual deserved to be honoured came about because a change had occurred that demanded it. If we define instinct as action *whose source is group-bound* then intentional action is action *whose source is in the individual*. At a point in time about 100,000 years ago there was a transition in human beings from instinctual action to intentional action. This transition increased the plasticity of human beings, which opened out their future technological ability, increasing their capacity to tailor the environment to their own needs. The sign of this new realization that we are intentional beings was the burial of the dead.

The burial of the dead was a religious act, an act of the group, and the recognition of the individual's intentionality. *A religious model of man then is one which posits that man is an intentional creature*. The model which is an antonym to this is the positivist model, which does not recognize this transition which occurred 100,000 years ago. It holds that man is a creature driven by instinct. It is a mistake to hold that the positivist view is scientific whereas the religious view is not. It is the job of science to determine which of these two views fits the facts best. Positivism does not recognize the reality of transformation. In this instance it does not recognize the transformation of instinctual action into ego-action.

The other positivist error is to misapply instinct theory. There is a level of explanation where its canons are appropriate. It is not that it is incorrect theoretically to say that man is driven by instincts. It is that it is not operating at the level of social emotional interaction; that at this level a different set of principles governs human behaviour within which the place of instincts is irrelevant. Imagine I am a journalist covering the election campaign in America and Bill Clinton walked out of his car across a piece of Tarmac and onto a podium, but instead of describing the speech that he made or his reception by the crowd I say that he could not have walked from his car to the podium unless there had been solid earth to walk upon and I go on to describe how the crust of the earth came to be and the formation of the American continent and that without this having

51

happened there could be no American election, no people in America, no evolution of mammalian life. All this would be perfectly correct but would have no relevance. It is not the level of explanation that is required. The editor of my newspaper would give me the sack. Instinct theory is of that nature. Its explanatory power is not relevant for the sphere of human activity with which we are concerned. It was, I believe, relevant prior to the *burial climax*.

What of Haeckel's view that ontogeny recapitulates phylogeny? This would mean that traces of our evolutionary development remain and therefore in the instance we are considering it would mean that instinctual drivenness remains in the personality. We need to frame this question within the paradigm that instinctual action is group-driven and intentional action is through individual choice. The notion that the individual regresses within the group seems well established and argued for convincingly by Freud in *Group Psychology and the Analysis of the Ego*, by Le Bon in his book *La Foule* and also by Bion in *Experiences in Groups*. However the evidence that stares us in the face is the manner in which a whole mass of people renounced their individual judgement in Nazi Germany and this has been repeated in Soviet Russia and Communist China. In such cases individuals are reduced to units in a system. However the fact that in such cases there have always been a few heroic individuals who have stood against the tide suggests that this regression to instinct does not happen automatically but that the individual is able to choose not to do it. In the group situation there is a pressure to regress to instinct and yet the fact that there is the possibility of choice means regression to instinct is not the same as for humans driven by instinct prior to that step when the tribal group started to bury their dead. The fact of choice alters its character. In the regression to instinct we are not in the same position as our hominid ancestors prior to the *burial climax* because in the regression there is the choice to refuse our humanness of today. This radically alters its character.

It seems that to refuse what we are, to refuse what we are able to become, does not reduce us to the level of the beasts but to something much worse. In common parlance we often speak of someone behaving like an animal or say that someone is a real brute but it invariably means a determined behaviour that is far worse than that of an animal. The savagery of a Hitler is far worse than the worst depredations of an animal. An eagle or a lion for instance kills because it needs food. Its depredations are tied to its instinct for survival whereas in a Hitler it is a passion that has no 'reason'. It is a spiritual passion that is unhitched from 'reason'. Subsequent to man's detachment from instinct he is a roving spirit based on choices. The savagery of a Hitler is not an instinctual matter but a spiritual passion. This is one of the reasons why analyses of the Nazi phenomenon by social scientists fail to grasp its essential nature. It cannot be explained within a positivist paradigm. Spiritual passion can be heroically good or diabolically evil.

We have already seen how detachment from the sensual is no guarantee of goodness, but rather signals the release of a spirituality which can lead either to heights of goodness or depths of evil. These two categories of goodness and evil are our way of describing the differential nature of spiritual choices. Therefore the question whether Haeckel's principle of ontogeny recapitulating phylogeny is a valid one has ultimately to be answered in the negative. The fact that it does not just 'happen', but choice enters into it, transforms the level of operation so that man can never be back to where he was. If he returns there it is an action, a choice, which it was not before the *burial climax*.

So the emergence of religion occurred in two distinct though connected events in the evolution of man. These two events were separated by a time lapse of some 60,000 to 100,000 years. The mentality heralded by the first we have designated as 'primitive' where physical survival was the central motivating principle. The mentality heralded by the second which I have designated 'mature' was a further detachment from instinct and transformation of mentality where meaning is found to exist in an action pattern that transcends the survival instinct. I have emphasized these two different mentalities because although these have been central in many anthropological researches and in religious studies departments, their import has been almost entirely ignored within psychoanalysis. Both Freud and Jung had no grasp of this distinction and yet it is crucial to our understanding not only of religion but also of psychoanalysis. The only exception that I know of is Erich Fromm, to whom we devote a chapter later. I believe the problem is that most social scientists working within a truncated Darwinism are themselves therefore operating within the schema of primitive mentality.

REFERENCES

Richard Leakey and Roger Lewin (1979) *People of the Lake* (London: Collins).
Karl Marx (1843) *Introduction to the Critique of Hegel's Philosophy of Religion* (Harmondsworth: Pelican Marx Library).
Colin Turnbull (1984) *The Forest People* (London: Triad/Paladin Books), p. 102.

PART TWO

In this section I review the psychoanalytic writings on religion. It is not comprehensive, but I hope sufficient to illustrate its main themes. By sifting through some of the main currents of this literature I aim to show why it has largely failed to elucidate the spiritual function of psychoanalysis.

8

Freud's Diagnosis of Religion

Impersonal forces and destinies cannot be approached; they remain eternally remote. But if the elements have passions that rage as they do in our own souls, if death itself is not something spontaneous but the violent act of an evil will, if everywhere in nature there are Beings around us of a kind that we know in our own society, then we can breathe freely, can feel at home in the uncanny and deal by psychical means with our senseless anxiety.

(Freud, 1927)

In this chapter, I shall examine *The Future of an Illusion*, which attends principally to the psychological origins of primitive religion, and *Moses and Monotheism*, which is concerned with the development of mature religion. I shall use hypotheses from *Totem and Taboo* for the elucidation of Freud's theories in both of these works. The origin of religion is inextricably linked with the origin of civilization and therefore the theme of religion runs through many other of Freud's writings, especially *Civilization and Its Discontents*.

According to Freud, the origin of primitive religion lies in man's helplessness in the face of the forces of impersonal nature; the origin of mature religion lies in man's guilt which derives from parricide. In Freud's interpretation of religion parricide is a thread which runs through both the primitive and the mature. At the beginning of *The Future of an Illusion*, Freud states that, 'Every individual is virtually an enemy of civilization.' It derives from Freud's conviction that we are trapped between our voracious drives and a civilization that forbids their expression. The point to be noted here is that the drives continue to exist in their uncivilized state, and must be kept in subjection within. Without external coercion, Freud states, human beings would indulge their rapacious passions:

> If, then, one may take any woman one pleases as a sexual object, if one
> may without hesitation kill one's rival for her love or anyone else who

57

stands in one's way, if, too, one can carry off any of the other man's belongings without asking leave – how splendid, what a string of satisfactions one's life would be.

As these passions that rage in the soul are the manifestation of the drives, it means that their object is the personal inflation of the individual at the expense of others and that the prohibitions of civilization are against this self-inflation. Freud, however, believes that these greedy impulses are the only ones that exist, that they are based in the drives, and that even in the development of civilization they have not changed. One of these impulses is the desire to kill the father, and it is the guilt arising from this desire that triggers various prohibitions. Freud sees the taboo against killing the totem animal as a displacement of this, as are the sexual prohibitions which society imposes on the individual. But prohibition is always imposed against the original impulse.

There is a psychological experience frequently encountered in the consulting-room which has no place in Freud, who did not believe in the transformation of desire. I shall give an example of this experience. I was treating a man who was frequently unfaithful to his wife. He felt guilty about this, and used to say, 'I mustn't, I mustn't', but he would nevertheless do it. After much analysis, one day he said, 'I had a strange experience yesterday. You know I saw Martha at the office and I realized that I did not *want* to fuck her. I could see that she was attractive, but I did not desire her sexually.' He did not want to, not because civilization in the person of his super-ego was prohibiting him, but because he did not desire it; desire had its origin in his ego. He could truthfully say 'I do not want to' not out of fear, but out of personal desire.

For the sake of convenience, let us call such an experience 'ego transformation'. We shall need to examine later what is meant by the phrase 'not out of fear but out of personal desire', but suffice it to say here that this is a component of experience that has no place in Freud, and of which he appears to have no knowledge. Instead, he maintains that such a transformation of the ego does not occur. While most psychoanalysts have had patients who consciously affirm their commitment to truth, justice, and compassion but whose inner dispositions are utterly ruthless, they also frequently witness a transformation whereby what was initially a possession of the super-ego becomes a possession of the ego. In such an ego transformation the values that become part of the ego's structure are also the core values of mature religion: compassion, truth, and goodness.

It might be argued that Freud recognizes a transformation of inner desire in sublimation. I think, however, that Freud's term 'sublimation' is an exact equivalent of the sociological term 'legitimation': for instance, a sociologist would say that in a surgeon the sadistic impulse is 'legitimated' – but he could just as well say that it is 'sublimated'. In either case, what is meant is that the sadistic impulse is given a legitimate outlet, but the implication here is that the person remains sadistic in his inner desire. Therefore, sublimation does not comment upon the state of inner desire. The concept of sublimation is a piece of sociological analysis which is common in Freud.

For Freud the prohibitions of civilization derive from guilt, the origins of which are primaeval parricide. In *Totem and Taboo*, Freud puts forward his anthropological hypothesis that primitive man lived in hordes rather like the apes, and that they were ruled by a patriarchal father, as the gorilla group is ruled by the male silverback. The sons rose up against the father and slew him, and the guilt deriving from this murder is the source of civilization's prohibitions. It also means we have within us unalloyed drives whose goal is the inflation of the self at the expense of the other: ' . . . if, too, one can carry off any of the other man's belongings without asking leave – how splendid, what a string of satisfactions one's life would be.' Freud suggests that the satisfaction of these drives would be the ultimate in human fulfilment, and so he says, 'The decisive question is whether and to what extent it is possible to lessen the instinctual sacrifices imposed on men.' The idea that there can be any transformation of human ruthlessness is implicitly dismissed by Freud. The implication of his view is that the imposition of sacrifices leads to an attenuation of human happiness; he does not consider that such a denial is capable of freeing the individual's creative capacity. The clinical evidence for both such a capacity and its liberation through knowledge and desire is witnessed frequently in the consulting-room.

Freud associates religion with the interdicts of the super-ego. He does not allow for the possibility of a higher motivating principle, as expressed by the religious teachers in the Axial and post-Axial Eras. It is not that he did not act from a higher principle himself. For instance, in his paper on narcissism (1914) he says, 'A strong egoism is a protection against falling ill, but in the last resort we must begin to love in order not to fall ill, and we are bound to fall ill if, in consequence of frustration, we are unable to love.' But he did not allow such a principle to alter his constancy, hedonistic, and drive theories which were the only motivating principles permitted in Freud's metapsychology. He struggled to fit love into his theoretical system, and managed it by stating that on the basis of reciprocal exchange the love that a person gives is replaced by the love that he or she receives. Yet this principle is contradicted elsewhere. We can see, then, Freud struggling to maintain a higher principle while trying to keep it within his hedonistic/drive theory.

Freud's thinking is linked to the survival instinct, which is proper to primitive religion, yet he believed in love and in the pursuit of truth, which are principles proper to mature religion. Freud's definition of religion therefore is suitable only for primitive religion because he refused to consider these principles as religious values. In fact, they are the central values of mature religion.

Freud shares the Hobbesian view that only fear of an external authority restricts the majority of people from vicious acts:

> There are countless civilized people who would not shrink from murder or incest but who do not deny themselves the satisfaction of their avarice, their aggressive urges or their sexual lusts and who do not hesitate to injure other people by lies, fraud and calumny so long as they can remain unpunished for it.

Freud says the above is so of 'countless civilized people', but implies it is not so of everyone. This is already a different statement. Is it correct to call such people 'civilized'? It would seem more correct to call them 'people within civilization', and maintain the term 'civilized person' for one in whom there has been an ego transformation, i.e., one not governed by fear of punishment.

In the quote that opens this chapter, Freud says that the origin of religion lies in our anxiety in the face of helplessness in a world of impersonal forces.

> Impersonal forces and destinies cannot be approached; they remain eternally remote. But if the elements have passions that rage as they do in our own souls, if death itself is not something spontaneous but the violent act of an evil will, if everywhere in nature there are Beings around us of a kind that we know in our own society, then we can breathe freely, can feel at home in the uncanny and can deal by psychical means with our own senseless anxiety.

This is the kernel of Freud's theory. He goes on to say that the infant projects the same patterning on to its parents, particularly the father. The origin of religion lies in this 'senseless anxiety' and with these Beings it is possible to resort to psychical means to appease them. In face of the impersonal forces of nature we are helpless, so through primitive religious rituals and sacrifices, we believe we are able to control the unexpected. It then dawned on the wise men of old that Fate stood above the gods. The province of the gods, or Fate at a later time, receded with the growth in scientific knowledge. Morality then became the sphere of religious preoccupation, and moral precepts were credited with divine origin. Freud states that once God was a single person rather than a plethora of spirits, the individual could recreate in Him the protective father, who would shelter him from death with the promise of a future life. Out of this came the belief in oneself as the beloved child, the Chosen People, enjoying God's special protection. This revelation, says Freud, ' . . . laid open to view the father who had all along been hidden behind every divine figure as its nucleus.'

Freud is vague when he refers to the 'wise men of old', the pivotal figures of the Axial Era who transformed primitive into mature religion. Although he recognizes the transition from animistic religion to mono-theism, he endows the latter with primitive qualities. The difference between the two for Freud is between polytheism and monotheism. The focus of religion is in appeasing God, and this applies to primitive religion as well as to mature religion. Therefore he has not understood the crucial transformation which occurred in civilization during the Axial Era. He seems blind to the fact that a new morality was born.

What is common to all the great teachers of the Axial Era is that they taught a new humanitarian morality. Freud did not understand that in these teachers there was a transformation of desire: the Buddha did not embrace the moral life because it was imposed, but because he wanted to. There was no necessary internal connection between the new morality and monotheism, which can be just as primitive as animism. In fact, in Taoism and early Buddhism this morality was explicitly associated with atheism. *What distinguishes primitive from mature religion is the source of the psychological action.*

In *Totem and Taboo*, the root of religion lies in man's guilt; in *The Future of an Illusion* it lies in man's infantile helplessness and anxious terror. The mother has assumed a place in *The Future of an Illusion* which is nowhere to be found in *Totem and Taboo*. Freud says that the mother is the child's first object-love and first protector against undefined dangers which threaten from the external world. The state of helplessness is therefore an early infantile one in relation to the mother.

The father then takes over this protective role. In *Moses and Monotheism*, father again assumes pride of place, and mother is banished from sight. One assumes that once the transition to father has taken place the primordial murder occurs, with its attendant guilt. Freud then states that the proofs for religious ideas are very insubstantial, summarizing them thus: first, they deserve to be believed because they were believed by our primal ancestors; second, we have proofs which have been passed down from primaeval times; third, it is forbidden to raise the question of authentication.

Freud's colleague, Oskar Pfister, whom we shall consider in the next chapter, showed up Freud's ignorance of biblical criticism, theological reflection, and apologetics. If Freud had had any knowledge of these he could not have adduced arguments that are not worthy of an educated man, let alone such a scholar and genius as Freud. He says that religious ideas did not come about from experience or thinking, but that they are illusions – i.e., the fulfilment of our strongest and most urgent wishes that persist because the helplessness of the child continues throughout adulthood. Belief in religion, then, is a manifestation of an infantile transference which remains un-worked-through, and the religious mythology transfixes the individual in a state of emotional childhood. Freud does not allow for the possibility of a religion based upon adult experience, and he does not allow for a religion based upon a natural theology. In other words, a religion based upon our common human experience of the world and which does not depend upon any claims to a privileged revelation.

Freud's definition of religion included primitive religion and Judaism and Christianity but excluded all other forms. His critique of religion probably arose from a passionate hatred of Judaism and of Catholicism as he knew it in *fin-de-siècle* Vienna. The thought of a religion based upon reason was quite outside his thinking; there is an impassable gulf between religious faith and reason. The kind of religiosity Freud encountered was probably of the superstitious variety, which relied for its authentication on supernatural experiences that lay outside the scope of reason. He says at one point that the deistic concept of God believed by philosophers is only a dim shadow of the mighty personality of religious doctrines, but this shows an ignorance of the core religious attitude of the great religious teachers, which was one of profound concern for humankind and the meaning of life.

Freud argues that religion legitimizes the unresolved aspects of the Oedipus complex:

> It is an enormous relief to the individual psyche if the conflicts of its childhood arising from the father-complex – conflicts which it has never wholly overcome – are removed from it and brought to a solution which is universally accepted.

In order to become an adult, Freud states, the individual always has to pass through a neurosis – the Oedipal conflict – in the same way that humankind in its cultural development has had to pass through a neurotic stage. This neurosis is religion, a phase which has to be traversed on the journey towards scientific rationality.

If religion does no harm, then why not just let those who want to believe it be free to do so? For Freud religion is not neutral: it harms the mind by arresting intellectual development. It is better if people admit to themselves the full extent of their helplessness. Freud does not discuss the mechanism by which people rid themselves of their sense of helplessness through identifying with an omnipotent figure (I identify myself with God, and it is through this mechanism that I protect myself from knowledge of my own helplessness, the child in me). Instead, we need to educate people to enter the world and become adults: 'Men cannot remain children for ever, they must in the end go out into "hostile life".' We have to give up clinging. If I believe in God, I remain a child clinging to my mother or father, though I do not realize this is the case. Realizing our helplessness rather than denying it through erecting an illusory, protective parent is a central aim in psychoanalysis, and a successful working-through of the Oedipus complex achieves this.

Freud presents a cogent argument against his outlook in the mouth of a would-be opponent, who states that Freud's enthusiasm for a society based on rational principles is itself an illusion. Freud replies that there is a distinction between his illusion and the religious illusion: whereas his is capable of correction, the religious illusion is not: 'In the long run nothing can withstand reason and experience, and the contradiction which religion offers to both is all too palpable.' He ends this work with a hymn to science: 'Our science is no illusion. But an illusion it would be to suppose that what science cannot give us we can get elsewhere.' We shall see later that Freud's model underpinning science is itself dogmatic and inflexible.

Freud wrote *Moses and Monotheism* in three parts, beginning in the early 1930s and only finishing the last part when he had moved to London in 1938. His contention that Moses was not an Israelite but an Egyptian was offensive to Orthodox Jews, and the eminent Jewish orientalist Abraham Shalom Yahuda pleaded that he should not publish it. Freud had already published the first two parts in *Imago*, but now intended publishing the whole as a book. In times of such severe anti-Semitism, Jews felt it as a severe blow that Freud, such an eminent member of their race and culture, should deprive his fellow people of the supreme figure of their history. In view of this one must suppose that Freud had strong reasons for publishing the work.

In claiming that Moses was an Egyptian, Freud starts by showing that Mosheh (Moses) is an Egyptian word meaning 'child'. Quoting Rank's *The Myth of the Birth of the Hero*, Freud says that heroes or heroines are always given a fantastic birth. Before birth there is often a period of barrenness, and also a prophecy concerning the child. He or she is usually the child of aristocratic parents, who is then farmed out to be nurtured by animals or people of humble birth. Psychoanalysis tells us that the aristocratic and humble family are in fact two perceptions of the same family – the early perception being the 'aristocratic' one and the later the 'humble' one.

In the case of Moses, the child is of humble parents but adopted by aristocratic ones. Freud says that one fragment of the myth remains: the child survived in the face of powerful external forces. The point Freud does not make is that to the Jew, being born of the People of God was an aristocratic endowment of far greater moment than being born an Egyptian. Instead, Freud says it is the second family which is the real one in these myths, and so the Egyptian family was the real one to which Moses was born.

As an Egyptian, Freud argues, Moses imbibed the monotheistic religion in Egypt and then converted a tribe of Israelites. Extending through Egypt's long history, its religion was polytheistic except for the short reign of Amenophis IV, who introduced monotheism into Egypt – the first time this phenomenon appeared in the world. Freud posits that Moses was one of his disciples. The God was called Aten, and Amenophis was renamed Akhenaten. When Akhenaten died, his fanatical beliefs – which had been imposed with all the vehemence with which Mary Tudor imposed Catholicism in her English realm – were reversed by the priests. Moses, then still an ardent believer, looked with disappointment at his infidel realm, turning instead to a community of poor Semite slaves. As their leader, he led them out of Egypt to found a new kingdom in Canaan. There is a gap in time between Akhenaten and the supposed date of the Exodus, but Freud supposes that the religion of Aten was kept alive by a small but devoted band of believers.

In his desire to explain the origins of monotheism, instead of attributing the beginning of monotheism to Abraham as in the scriptures, Freud states that monotheism began with Akhenaten, who passed it on to Moses, who in turn converted the Israelites. Freud's account, however, does nothing to elucidate how monotheism came into being. It makes little difference whether we say monotheism started with Abraham or with Akhenaten; ultimately, who passed on this belief to the Israelites is of little consequence. What matters is the steadfastness of their belief, and what is of interest is how the idea of one god came into the mind of one man. How did he come by such a belief? What meaning did it have? Why did he espouse it with such fanatical certainty? Why were all other gods banished with such ferocity? None of this is answered by Freud.

There is, however, one psychological difference between Moses and Abraham which is extremely important, though it is not clear whether this was intended by Freud: Moses turns to convert the Israelites out of loneliness and disappointment, whereas Abraham goes forth in search of his god in a spirit of hope and adventure. It is difficult not to conclude that Freud's main purpose in claiming that Moses was an Egyptian was to dethrone the idol of his people.

Having established these facts, Freud then introduces the tradition, first hinted at in the prophet Hosea, that Moses was killed by his own people in Kadesh and the people reverted to the worship of idols. It was only later that monotheism was revivified, and in migratory waves over generations the Israelites colonized Canaan.

Freud has erected the murder of Moses into a place of supreme significance: it is racial parricide which produces guilt, out of which is born ethical monotheism. That civilization begins with a parricide is the thesis of the last part of *Totem and Taboo*. Freud returns to the same thesis and posits that Western civilization, deriving as it does from the Judaeo-Christian religion, is based upon guilt. Because this religion centres on appeasement, it is essentially the same in its psychological attitude as animism, which Freud discusses in *Totem and Taboo*. Guilt instigates the renunciation of instinct: the motive which lies behind renunciation is therefore guilt and the desire to appease.

Renunciation or detachment motivated by a desire to be free to love is not considered by Freud. He also makes no reference to those passages in the Prophets where humane behaviour is most earnestly sought:

> What I want is love, not sacrifice;
> knowledge of God, not holocausts.
>   (Hosea 6:6)

> I reject your oblations,
> I refuse to look at your sacrifices of fattened
>   cattle.
> Let me have no more of the din of your chanting,
> no more of your strumming harps.
> But let justice flow like water,

and integrity like an unfailing stream.

(Amos 5:22–24)

This is what Yahweh asks of you:
only this, to act justly,
to love tenderly
and to walk humbly with your God.

(Amos 6:8)

The ethical ideals expressed here are either implanted by God – as believed by many religious people – and dismissed by Freud, or they have to be explained within the hedonistic schema, which is in fact narcissistic: I only act so as to satisfy myself, therefore society can only function through imposing a severe sanction against such behaviour.

To summarize, what Freud condemns is primitive religion, which erects gods or a god to protect us against the impersonal, uncontrollable forces of nature. It explains the mysteries of nature as the creation of God, and therefore inhibits intellectual curiosity and prevents us working to discover the world around us. All religions, primitive and mature, come under this rubric for Freud. All religion arises out of guilt, and its activities are therefore geared to appeasement, sapping us of the energy which we need to manage our world. Freud does not attend to the matter of ethics except to see renunciation in this same pejorative light. That Freud believed in the central humanitarian ideals of mature religion is quite clear, but he did not associate these with religion. We need now to give attention to Meissner's recent critique of Freud and religion.

REFERENCES

S. Freud (1913) *Totem and Taboo*, Standard Edition (SE), vol. XIII.
— (1914) *On Narcissism: An Introduction*, SE, vol. XIV.
— (1927) *The Future of an Illusion*, SE, vol. XXI.
— (1930) *Civilization and Its Discontents*, SE, vol. XXI.
— (1939) *Moses and Monotheism*, SE, vol. XXIII.
P. Gay (1988) *A Life For Our Time* (London/Melbourne: J. M. Dent & Sons Ltd).

9

Meissner's Critique of Freud

Quite by the way, why did none of the devout create psychoanalysis? Why did one have to wait for a completely godless Jew?

(Freud, 1963)

The most comprehensive assessment of Freud's attitude to religion is to be found in W. W. Meissner's book *Psychoanalysis and Religious Experience*. Meissner examines Freud's arguments in his main texts on religion, and then in particular discusses the great debate on religion that took place between Freud and Oskar Pfister, a friend and colleague. In this chapter I shall look at this debate, and Meissner's perceptive commentary on it.

Freud published *The Future of an Illusion* in *Imago* in 1927, and Pfister published a reply the following year entitled *The Illusion of a Future*. Pfister, a Lutheran pastor working in a parish in Zurich, discovered Freud's writings in 1908 and from that moment became an enthusiastic disciple. Despite being a firm believer in the Christian faith, he and Freud remained firm friends. It was probably Pfister's unbounded respect for Freud's genius that enabled Freud to tolerate his friend's disagreement with his own religious position. Freud was thus pleased that it was Pfister who replied to his article against religion (the subtitle of Pfister's article is 'A friendly dispute with Prof. Dr. Sigm. Freud'). He knew his article would call forth replies from defenders of religious faith, and this being the case, a reply from Pfister was more welcome than from some other quarter, which would probably be more hostile.

Pfister starts his article by saying that the cult of totems is based on different determinants from those of the ethical monotheism of the Prophets. He is here referring to the distinction which I have emphasized between primitive and mature religion, though not making it as clear. He is correct in pointing out the way in which Freud sees the origin of Jewish monotheism as having the same determinant as totemism: i.e., parricide. Pfister goes on to say that the formation of restraints, which was so emphasized by Freud, is not inherent in religion; quite the contrary, as the 'highest religions', as he puts it, remove restraint. He says that the religion of Jesus assails the kind of legalism about which Freud complains. Pfister emphasizes that new freedom is given in the Christian faith, and that Jesus placed love at the centre of his religion. Jesus gets beneath the symptoms to the underlying moral–religious conflict, thereby preceding psycho-analysis by 1,900 years.

Pfister stresses that God is not a god to be placated in the religion of Jesus, but rather to be loved humanly in our neighbour. He suggests that the Protestant principle of freedom is a message of liberation from not only religious compulsion, but all compulsions. He sees the development of religion as a process of humanization, and so denies outright that neurotic compulsive character traits are inherent in religion. I believe they are inherent in primitive religion, but not in mature religion.

Pfister says that while many elements of religion are the products of wish-fulfilment, this does not account for religion altogether; atheism also is frequently the product of wish-fulfilment. Religion is not the fulfilment of egoistic wishes, and in fact the religion of Jesus is in direct opposition to egoism. In the state of nature the individual is egoistic, and Christian teaching specifically challenges this position.

Pfister states that wishful thinking has played a large part in scientific theorizing as well as in religion. Although Freud acknowledges this at the end of *The Future of an Illusion*, he does not give it sufficient weight, apparently assuming that scientific theory is free of wish-fulfilment. Pfister says Freud idealizes science, and his scientific approach is divorced from philosophy – a criticism also made by Jung. In essence Pfister is saying that Freud is naïve in his idolization of science: 'Natural science without metaphysics does not exist, never did exist and never will exist.'

However, Pfister does not answer Freud's main challenge in this matter: that religious dogmas are rigid and do not give way in the face of new evidence in the way that scientific hypotheses do, or are able to do. According to Pfister, Freud replaces feelings, wishes and values with intellect. Moral life cannot be left to conscience alone, which Freud seems to suggest. He also says there are other issues central to religion which are not even mentioned by Freud, for instance the meaning and value of life.

He challenges Freud's view that religion arrests intellectual develop-ment, naming a long list of philosophers, scientists, historians, artists and statesmen who were highly intelligent as well as being religious. Freud's idea that religion is a compensation for misery here below, Pfister claims, is a misunderstanding of Christianity.

Meissner points out that Freud's view of human nature is pessimistic, and quotes one of Freud's letters to Pfister:

> I do not break my head very much about good and evil, but I have found little that is 'good' about human beings on the whole. In my experience most of them are trash, no matter whether they publicly subscribe to this or that ethical doctrine or to none at all.

I think 'pessimistic' is too mild a word to describe the sentiments expressed here. It seems clear that Freud's attitude, as in other places in his writings, is downright contemptuous. Meissner points out that Pfister is much more optimistic about human nature, and goes on to say that 'The contrasting attitudes and spirit of the two thinkers provided the omnipresent background that subtly but inexorably influenced the course and tenor of their debate.' In neither thinker, however, is there apparent that intense struggle between good and evil which characterizes those who have put spiritual affairs at the forefront of their lives; in Freud we find sombre negativism, and in Pfister a somewhat naïve optimism. What is most characteristic of the two men is a dogmatic adherence to their own doctrine. Pfister says, 'There is not much danger of your turning up for baptism or of my descending from the pulpit.' This statement characterizes the debate: neither is going to move on the issue. There might be some accommodation of matters of secondary importance, but no possibility of a new synthesis arising, which can only mean there will be no truly creative outcome. Such rigid positioning runs through all the debates between psychoanalysis and religion, even with analysts who are sympathetic to religion. The two spheres remain in parallel, without any true synthesis.

Meissner starts by saying that psychoanalysis has tended to see religious experience in psychopathological terms, and then that religious and theological reflection has tended to ignore human drives and needs. It is, I believe, unfortunate that in the opening chapter he sees the dichotomy in this way, apparently accepting that Freud's model of drives and needs is correct. As we have seen, the drive model does not do justice to the intentional nature of human beings, which is an explanatory prerequisite of all mature religions.

Meissner differentiates between religion founded on a healthy base and one founded on a neurotic structure, making this parallel:

The situation is not much different from that of the patient who is troubled by an unsatisfactory marital relationship. If the relationship is based on neurotic components, the analytic effort, in so far as it serves to expose these components and resolve the underlying issues, will lead to the dissolution of the marriage. Where elements of solid and meaningful relationship, love, and mutual respect can be identified, the expunging of neurotic contaminants can only strengthen that relationship.

He creates a dichotomy between what is religious and what is human. Psychology can study the human behaviour and experience, but has no authority over revelation and the supernatural experience. He also says that the religious convictions of the psychologist should not influence his or her psychological understanding, but in fact convictions, whether religious or otherwise, *do* influence psychological understanding. Only on the basis of splitting – a mechanism which psychoanalysis attempts to repair – can a psychologist have a powerful belief or conviction which does not influence psychological understanding. He therefore equates religion with divine revelation, over which psychology – and philosophy for that matter – can have no authority. In this way Meissner gives no place to natural theology, which is the possibility of religious experience understood by the light of reason alone (the only writer on psychoanalysis and religion who does give natural theology a place is Erich Fromm, whom we shall consider later; it is surprising that Meissner makes no mention of Fromm).

Meissner does say that love and mutual respect are crucial components of religious experience. He introduces, then, a dichotomy between a god who is totally unknowable, beyond the realm of human understanding, and the human world. This means there is no base for religion within human affectivity, and ultimately divorces morality from religion. Freud's claim that religious belief is fideist, belief on the basis of *credo quia absurdum*, finds justification in the approach to religion which Meissner takes: that is, to limit religion to revealed religion, as Meissner does, substantiates the *credo quia absurdum*.

The problem is that a religious conviction based on revelation is by definition divorced from reason, which is a crucial component of human experience. A psychoanalyst who has a religious conviction based on revelation rather than reason is condemned to split his religious beliefs and his scientific outlook. While Christian apologetics has always maintained that nothing in Christian revelation is contrary to reason, this does not alter the fact that what is proposed can only be accepted with conviction through a special, supernatural gift from God.

I believe Freud was particularly taking issue with a religion based on revelation, so, for instance, Meissner says, 'Freud's limitation was that he was not a believer, and that he held fixed and prejudicial ideas about the role of religion in human life, so that he could not be an objective or perceptive observer of it.' One could argue, though, that Freud was a very perceptive observer of revealed religion. Meissner gives no place for any religion other than revealed religion. His book is about the Judaeo-Christian religious tradition, and in particular Catholicism.

From remarks at the end of the book, however, Meissner is aware that there are large areas that he has not addressed. Although Meissner correctly points out that Freud's view of religion is reductionistic through his use of the analogy of obsessional neurosis, which Meissner rightly says is just one aspect of religion, it is also the case that Meissner's view of religion has a narrow focus; it may be for this reason that he makes no mention of Fromm, whose view of religion was much wider.

That Meissner addresses the thesis that Freud presents in *Moses and Monotheism* reflects that Meissner is probably the only psychoanalyst past or present who has a thorough knowledge of biblical scholarship. He begins by acknowledging that,

> Certain elements do suggest a possible relationship to the worship of Aten. One such element is the concept of a god who is the sole creator of all things. Another is the emphasis on one god and the recognition that such a deity must necessarily be international, cosmic and universal.

However, Meissner tends to the view that the concept of Yahweh was slowly built up by a sort of accretion of the tribal gods. This seems more probable than Freud's idea that the Israelites were converted to monotheism by Moses, and that the religion died with him and then was 'remembered' and revived many generations later. Meissner thinks this syncretistic process was deepened by the intervention of Moses. Moses lived some four centuries before the Axial Era. The emphasis he brought to the religion was that of the covenant between Yahweh and the People – a demand that they be faithful to their God as a communal group. Freud's interpretation of how the Israelites adopted monotheism is more miraculous than the saner, scientific account given by Meissner, who states that unconditional monotheism was only established in Israel at the time of the Prophets, and whether this can be attributed to Moses is doubtful. The religion of Moses only tended towards monotheism; the attribution of unconditional monotheism to Moses was the work of a much later redaction. Meissner's sums up Freud's position in these words:

> Specifically in terms of Freud's historical suppositions, our review of the evolution of the Israelite religious traditions suggests that his hypothesis – that a pure Egyptian monotheism was imposed on the Jewish people as a replacement for their primitive polytheism, which was subsequently repressed and later emerged as the worship of Yahweh – cannot be maintained in the face of contemporary views of biblical history. A more realistic view suggests that the seminomadic Hebrews derived their religious traditions from Mesopotamian roots, evolving the worship of a specific deity by each clan from a polytheistic matrix of belief. The emergence of Moses on this scene was a brilliant moment of religious insight and perhaps revelation. But the monotheism of Moses remains ambiguous and presents itself as continuous with the extant context of Hebraic belief. Moreover, the moral code that accompanies the Yahwistic formulas of Mosaic doctrine has stronger parallels in non-Egyptian sources.

It is paradoxical that it is Freud, the passionate unbeliever, who proposes a more fantastic and less rational origin for monotheism than the more sober religious scholars of the Bible. It is difficult to understand what Freud hoped to gain by attributing the Israelites' adoption of monotheism to their conversion by an Egyptian Moses.

Meissner goes on to discuss the ways in which the image of God is formed in childhood and adolescence, concluding this account by saying, 'Freud's account can be seen as presenting critical insight into a narrow range of the dynamics of belief, artificially isolated from the full range and complexity of human religious experience.' For Meissner, the concept of God is laid down during the early mirroring phase. At about six months the child begins to get a sense of itself through apprehending and internalizing its own reflection. The first formulation of this was by Jacques Lacan, who thought of the literal reflection which the child saw in a mirror. Later Winnicott developed this further to mean the sense that the child gets of itself from 'seeing itself' in the mother's response to it. We believe that Meissner meant it in the sense in which Winnicott understood it. If the mirroring phase has been defective, the individual will become omnipotent – a feeling of being *like* God instead of being *with* God. The child then passes on to a stage of dependence on an idealized maternal imago, around which his or her notion of God is shaped.

From this time onwards the child's concept of God is coloured by parental and family influences. I do not agree with Meissner's formulation of the bad mother – the child's fantasy of destruction and being devoured, promoted by a real mother who is not able to satisfy infantile wishes – because it does not give sufficient weight to the infant's intentional structuring of the environment. One can see here the confusion that results from accepting Freud's deterministic model and rejecting the libertarian one, yet Meissner accepts unquestioningly Freud's deterministic model with its associated drive theory. This is surprising, in view of the fact that he generally attempts to support the religious view of man.

Meissner believes in an auto-erotic stage followed by one of primary narcissism. The analysts of the object relations school will not agree with this formulation, and as he links primary narcissism with mystical experience, they will have to find another explanatory schema for mysticism. On the other hand, Meissner categorizes God as a transitional object that is created, and so in this sphere posits an intentional structuring, although he does not posit that the transitional object is the structuring agent: he incorporates Winnicott's view without the modification required by his phenomenological standpoint.

The individual's God representation is private, expressed in prayer, and not reconcilable with the God of scripture, theology or philosophy: 'The individual believer prays to a God who is represented by the highly personalized transitional object representation in his inner, private, personally idiosyncratic belief system.' There is thus a dichotomy between the individual's representation, and the conceptualizations of scripture and theology. I am surprised by this dichotomy between private and communal belief. Probably the most significant contribution made by the liturgical movement which swept through the Christian churches in the 1950s and 1960s was to emphasize that the piety of the individual Christian is that of the whole Christian body. Jewish prayer is also a private appropriation of what is essentially the worship of God's People. The thinking of the liturgical movement was that piety divorced from the communal structure of belief tended towards sentimentality. In contradistinction to Freud, Meissner says it would be as wrong to tear someone from this God representation as to tear a child from his teddy bear. This, however, does not answer Freud's point: that religion is sought as a consolation in the face of helplessness.

In his exposition of transitional phenomena, there is some confusion when Meissner states that illusion stands between the subject and reality, as if there were some independent reality that is not constructed. But what if all reality is precisely such a construction? Then we need another criterion to differentiate between the real and the unreal. The failure of this sort of argument is that its focus is upon the idea of God, whereas the kernel of mature religion is in moral action. The differentiation between the real and unreal in human affairs lies in the quality of moral action. In an analysis of the real it is necessary to differentiate between the non-human reality studied by the natural sciences and the human reality studied by the human sciences.

Meissner makes the point that Freud's neurological model was a reactive one, whereas modern neurological research shows that the neural system propagates neural impulses, and that levels of energic processing bear no relation to motivational states. He chooses a hermeneutic model of psychoanalysis, therefore ruling out the natural science model of psycho-analysis. In phenomenology, he states, intentionality becomes the defining characteristic of psychic life, and he here follows this view. It seems that what Meissner says about reality when discussing transitional phenomena contradicts the position he maintains in most of his book. I believe he slips into these contradictions because the intentional view he espouses demands that he banish the deterministic theory of Freud – but this he does not do. That Meissner takes intentionality as central is stated clearly: 'Ultimately, then, in both a philosophical and psychoanalytic perspective, intentionality is fundamental to the whole of psychic life.'

He points out further that intentionality is not merely cognitive but extends to 'all aspects of human relatedness', extending to objects and persons. Freud's hedonistic theory is a 'closed system' in this sense. However, although mature religion has been wedded to a theory of intentionality, this has been restricted to consciousness. Meissner states that today psychoanalysis encompasses wider spheres of conscious life, such as adaptation and conflict-free areas of the ego.

I believe that intentionality in psychoanalysis and religion are much more similar than Meissner realizes. He comes close to the idea that conscious and unconscious intentionality are much closer together than is generally conceived:

> Thus, the philosophical, phenomenological approach radically reverses the psychoanalytic dichotomy between conscious and unconscious mental processes. It sets itself against the proposition that the unconscious is the true reality and that conscious acts can only be explained or understood when reduced to parallel unconscious processes. Rather, both the conscious and unconscious are seen as participating in the same order of reality and significance.

By adhering to the unconscious as a separate sphere of the mind, Meissner has erected an obstacle in the absence of which he would find the religious and psychoanalytic model of the mind much closer. The unconscious is fashioned through repression, and, as Freud pointed out, repression is the *withdrawal* of psychic attention from a particular sphere of the mind. This sphere is the agent which acts immorally towards objects, i.e., the bad. The ego therefore *creates* a sphere of unconsciousness based on the Socratic principle that I cannot do evil and know it; therefore I split it off, or in other words, fashion the unconscious. Thus the unconscious is most emphatically a religious concept.

When he discusses free will and determinism, Meissner says that psychoanalysis has loosened the deterministic connection. However, he does not get to the root of freedom because he does not analyse freedom from the moral perspective – that moral action is essentially free because it implies acting for a motive that transcends the survival instinct, and that such a theory of moral action is required to make sense of intentionality, which psychoanalysis elucidates through interpretation. Unfortunately, Meissner, like so many, equates determinism with the scientific. At this point the reader is left in some confusion, because he then states that, 'Psychoanalysis is ultimately a natural science and cannot escape the demands of a natural science methodology.'

Meissner takes the view of traditional Catholic apologetics that psycho-analysis is not in contradiction to the claims of Catholicism. He does not allow for the possibility, however, that psychoanalysis is a morality – indeed a spirituality – that demands a revision of Christian dogma and moral attitudes. It is, I believe, because psychoanalysis is a spirituality founded on reason, therefore offering itself as a substitute for revealed religion, that Meissner must keep it safely as a natural science where it can do no harm.

When he comes to discuss morality, Meissner makes an error because he seems to identify morality with moralizing. Standing as an analyst in the view that drive-derived behaviour is moral is in contradiction to what Meissner says earlier about intentionality. Intentional action towards objects is necessarily moral. We may wish that it were not, but it is.

For Meissner, psychoanalysis inhabits the human sphere, the sphere of natural science, whereas religion is a God-given gift: 'One either accepts the religious perspective through faith and embraces the religious belief system, or one does not.' In one fell swoop this statement discounts the possibility of religious action at the unconscious emotional level, and also justifies Freud's *credo quia absurdum* as the basis of all religious belief. Nevertheless, Meissner's book remains a valuable work, especially his

elucidation of the Freud–Pfister debate, and his scholarly examination of
the origins of monotheism.

REFERENCES

S. Freud (1963) *Psycho-Analysis and Faith: The Letters of Sigmund Freud and Oskar
Pfister* (London: The Hogarth Press).
W. W. Meissner (1983) *Psychoanalysis and Religious Experience* (New Haven and
London: Yale University Press).

10

The Challenge of Jung

Among all my patients in the second half of life . . . there has not been one whose problem in the last resort was not that of finding a religious outlook on life. It is safe to say that every one of them fell ill because he had lost that which the living religions of every age have given to their followers, and none of them has been really healed who did not regain his religious outlook.

(Jung, 1984)

There are so many contradictions in Jung that it is difficult to present his views in a coherent way. I shall try to lay bare the contradictions as they appear.

Jung outlines his approach to religion in his long article 'Psychology and Religion'. The foremost contradiction is his conceptualization of the relation of the human subject to the object world. On the one hand, Jung says that facts are facts, and they impress themselves on the mind *as they are*; on the other hand, facts are the product of imaginary construction. One moment he is a strict empiricist in the tradition of Locke, and the next moment he is a constructionist in the school of Kant. It is the empiricist view, however, that predominates in Jung's analysis of religion, and his definition is consistent with this viewpoint:

> Religion, as the Latin word denotes, is a careful and scrupulous observation of . . . the *numinosum*, that is: a dynamic agency or effect not caused by an arbitrary act of will. On the contrary, it seizes and controls the human subject, who is always rather its victim than its creator.

The position taken in this book is that a religion that is relevant to our lives in the social structures that are dominant in the modern world is one of human construction through the assistance of reason. Jung's position is the extreme opposite of this: essentially, the person's role is to submit to the power of an outer fact – the *numinosum* – which grips hold of the psyche. One can imagine that an extreme masochism could be the result of such a submission – a crushing of the self. My experience as an analyst tells me that when someone lives in a crushed state – whether it be a woman crushed by her husband, a man crushed by his boss, or a person crushed by the social system of which he is a part – its cause is to be found in the workings of a savage super-ego which functions unconsciously. What Jung attributes to an outer reality is attributed by object relations theorists to an inner reality, the savage super-ego, which is projected into an external object.

Jung is on record as stating not only that he believes in God's existence but that he *knows* that God exists. I do not want to argue here whether a rational proof for God's existence or non-existence is possible, which requires an epistemological analysis, followed by an ontological investigation, which is outside the scope of this book and my capacities. Among those who believe in the existence of an Absolute Being there is an enormous difference in the individual's emotional perception of it. Caryll Houselander said, 'The greatest fallacy is that we all worship the same God.'

Jung's perception of the *numinosum* is of a being who 'seizes and controls the human subject'. This is precisely the way a savage super-ego functions in the personality. The aim of the Kleinian psychoanalyst Herbert Rosenfeld, as demonstrated in some of his clinical papers, was to reduce the power of this super-ego. Jung, however, counsels submission to it.

There is, however, a moral dilemma here. It is a fact of clinical observation that an individual functioning in submission to a savage super-ego is, unbeknown to himself, tyrannizing emotionally those of his microsocial environment secondarily, and primarily his own selfhood. Knowing this, does the analyst allow such a patient to continue in ignorance of this activity? It seems that Jung was not aware of this level of emotional moral functioning, but whether he was or not he recommends to some patients that they return to their traditional religious 'home':

> If the patient is a practising Catholic I invariably advise him to confess and to receive communion in order to protect himself from immediate experience, which might easily prove too much for him.

Every experienced clinician would agree with Jung that if individuals have been existing with the belief that they have had a traumatized upbringing, are being exploited by their boss at work, and are not loved or appreciated by their partner, it comes as a great shock to discover that they have alienated their parents, exasperated their boss, and estranged their partner. Many clinicians, however, would disagree with Jung's policy of protecting such a person from the experience. An experienced clinician will, like a skilled craftsman, work away at the belief slowly so that the 'immediate experience' can be integrated bit by bit over time. I am not saying that this is easy, or not dangerous, but there are also hazards in seeking protection from danger.

The individual who seeks protection rather than facing a danger condemns him- or herself to emotional stasis. They opt against emotional growth; ultimately this means that the psychic illness – the neurosis or psychosis – is walled off and protected rather than disclosed, understood, and analysed. On the social side, is a religion or religious denomination growing in social effectiveness if its neophytes seek membership for protection? If this is the case, is it surprising that traditional religions cease to have relevance in today's world full of dangers, horrors, and emotional catastrophes of the worst kind?

Jung presents us with another, related problem in that he identifies objective existence with what is believed by the majority: 'Psychological existence is subjective in so far as an idea occurs only in one individual. But it is objective in so far as that idea is shared by a society – by a *consentium gentium*.' Jung infers that the *numinosum*, the outer reality, is identical with the *consentium gentium*, which in its turn is an objective reality. The idea that objectivity is to be identified with an idea that is shared by the many is a dangerous principle upon which to proceed. One has only to think of the way in which a whole society believed in Hitler's ideal during the Second World War. Gordon Zahn in his book *German Catholics and Hitler's Wars* points out how the whole Catholic hierarchy supported Hitler's war aims and that on the occasion of the fall of France High Mass was celebrated by the Catholic bishops in most of the cathedrals of Germany to offer thanks for this great victory. I take this example in illustration of the fact that the general thrust of Hitler's ideals was supported by a whole society. Jung seemed to be unaware that there can be a *folie à millions*, as Fromm emphasizes. This fits Jung's theory of archetypes, whereby an idea can take possession of populations quite independently of the creative function of individuals; it also seems that he reveres a religion of this kind.

Jung equates the truth with what exists, reducing it to what is applicable to the inanimate world, but not necessarily appropriate for the human world. This approach allows no space for a human definition of truth. Using Jung's definition, it would be necessary to conclude that Fascism is true because it exists, rather than recognize that the truth in human affairs is constituted by judgement. Jung, however, will not allow judgement to be a determinant of truth or reality. His definition of the *numinosum*, and therefore of religion, has this same empiricist bias:

The *numinosum* – whatever its cause may be – is an experience of the subject independent of his will. At all events, religious teaching as well as the *consentium gentium* always and everywhere explains this experience as being due to a cause external to the individual. The *numinosum* is either a quality belonging to a visible object or the influence of an invisible presence that causes a peculiar alteration of consciousness.

This view is clearly favourable to religions which stake their claim upon an outside agency being the originator of their beliefs. It therefore fits particularly well into the doctrinal schema of Judaism, Christianity and Islam. The most lucid instance of the *numinosum* as Jung defines it would be the ecstatic seizures during which the Prophet Muhammad was gripped by the power of Allah. It follows that the religious experience embodied within Islam would be an ideal type for Jung. Within Christianity, Jung favours Catholicism because it is less invested with subjectivism than Protestantism, which is why the Catholic Church has always favoured Jung rather than Freud. In Catholic theology, God's grace is made available in the sacraments whether or not the recipient is worthy or in the right state of mind. Jung's understanding of religion legitimizes religious attitudes that are authoritarian; from here it is a small step to ideological tyranny. His conceptualization of religion bypasses reason and human judgement.

The *numinosum* is an empirical fact and human consciousness is changed by it, Jung therefore believes the individual is not responsible for his psychic illnesses: 'If a man is suffering from a real cancer, he never believes himself to be responsible for such an evil, despite the fact that the cancer is in his own body.' Jung then goes on to say the following:

> But when it comes to the psyche we instantly feel a kind of responsibility, as if we were makers of our psychic conditions. This prejudice is of relatively recent date. Not so very long ago even highly civilized people believed that psychic agencies could influence our minds and feelings . . . in former times the man with the idea that he had cancer . . . would probably have assumed that somebody had worked witchcraft against him or that he was possessed. He never would have thought of himself as the originator of such a fantasy.

From my experience, this is not true. A man who discovered he had cancer said, 'I know I have brought this on myself'. Even more do people feel they have brought upon themselves psychological ills. It is a matter of clinical observation that the body can become a vessel into which hated inner experiences are discharged. For example, when an analyst went on holiday, a female patient said it was quite all right, it made no difference to her – but during that time she developed pneumonia. On each occasion that the analyst concurred with the statements of her false self, some bodily condition erupted. It seems that Jung is asking us to consider that these conditions might be caused by wizards, witches, demons or angels, that there are autonomous personalities within the psyche with a mental life of their own – but he does not have a theory as to their genesis. This view of religion is at the opposite pole to that taught and practised by the Buddha, who believed that many of the ills that befall us are a consequence of our own actions.

Jung's emphasis that in each individual there are within the psyche autonomous personalities is certainly a good analytic technique whereby the individual is made aware of such personalities functioning within, and that they shall do battle with those which are damaging their psychological well-being. However, his insistence that the individual has no responsibility for these is gainsaid by this author's own experience.

The strange contradiction in Jung is that on the one hand he states that his approach is empirical, and yet he produces a theory of religion which borders on the superstitious – there is no scientific attempt to explain the *numinosum*, or the demons and angels in whose existence he seems to believe. He just states in a dogmatic way that these things exist.

One of the most exasperating features of Jung's argumentation is his flat denial of his own value judgements. For instance, in one sentence he says, 'Protestantism has, in the main, lost all the finer shades of traditional Christianity: the mass, confession, the greater part of the liturgy, and the vicarious function of priesthood.' Then in the very next he says, 'I must emphasize that this statement is not a value-judgement and not intended to be one. I merely state the facts.' Yet when he says that Protestantism has lost all the 'finer' shades of traditional Christianity, what is that if not a value judgement? Another person might say that it was the 'baser' aspects that were lost.

Jung's insistence on there being no value judgement when there is so clearly one being made makes one distrust his other categorical statements. For instance, when he says of a series of dreams that, 'They represent an entirely uninfluenced natural sequence of events', it makes one suspicious, especially when he then comments on the dream by saying that, 'The first part of the dream is a serious statement in favour of the Catholic church. A certain Protestant point of view – that religion is just an individual experience – is discouraged by the dreamer.'

Dreams are profoundly influenced by the transference, which was clearly an important factor in this dreamer's relationship to Jung. Yet although he has let the reader know that this is *his* view of religion, he states categorically that the dreams were uninfluenced. Given that Jung favours Catholicism over the dreamer's bias of Protestantism, it stretches credibility that the dreamer was 'entirely uninfluenced'.

Jung does not allow for any intentional factors in the construction of a dream: 'I dare not make any assumptions about its possible cunning or its tendency to deceive. The dream is a natural occurrence . . . .' And in another place he says, '*I take the dream for what it is*' [his italics]. In other words, the dream is the expression of an autonomous personality. There is no construction, no value judgement, or judgement at all.

An autonomous personality may arise in the following way, using the previous patient cited as an example. The patient functions as a child in the inner core of her personality. She says she is looking forward to the coming holiday, but when the analyst goes away she collapses with pneumonia. During the following break she develops hepatitis, and one break after another she succumbs to illnesses of different kinds. Her behaviour is governed by a cynical, sneering attitude that she is all right, that it does not trouble her that the analyst is going away, and so on. As the analysis proceeds, it becomes clear that she is governed from within by a harsh stepmother who shuts away the child as the witch did in Hansel and Gretel. It is this stepmother/witch who takes over in the analyst's absence. From reconstruction, it is probable that this personality took over when in infancy this patient lost her mother, and her father remarried when she was about three. This stepmother/witch did not take over when the analyst went on holiday as a stimulus-response reaction, but rather the patient, feeling betrayed, turned away from the analyst in great bitterness. This personality therefore, is an individual human creation.

That there is a strong predisposition to move in this direction and that this is strengthened by trauma I have no doubt, but the personal element in its creation *and* in its continued existence is something which Jung seems to dismiss entirely. My own contention is that the *numinosum* is also created in this way and, further, that submission to it keeps the person at the infantile stage of development.

The core values which were preached by the great religious teachers – the Buddha, Jesus and Socrates – were a radical challenge to the mentality of primitive religion. Jung accepts the tenets of primitive religion; it seems he endorses or is protective of the primitive state of mind, and shrinks from encouraging his patients to take the step towards an emotionally responsible moral position. He does not seem to be fully aware of the gigantic step that was taken by those initiators of mature religion. Neither Freud nor Jung understood that there is a religion of a more mature kind; the difference between the two is that Freud condemns primitive religion uncompromisingly, whereas Jung gives it his support.

REFERENCES

Isaiah Berlin (1979) 'The Divorce between the Sciences and the Humanities' in *Against the Current* (London: The Hogarth Press), p. 96.

C. G. Jung (1984) *Modern Man in Search of a Soul* (London, Melbourne and Henley: Ark Paperbacks/Routledge & Kegan Paul), p. 264.

Gordon Zahn (1963) *German Catholics and Hitler's Wars* (London: Sheed & Ward).

11

From Causal to Moral in Psychoanalysis

Freud's mechanistic and causal language stands in the way of a proper appreciation of his aims and achievements.

(Dilman, 1984)

It is the Judaeo-Christian view that God created man, and that this act was the goal of creation in order that man might share in the beneficent goodness of God's life. The universe is subordinate to this purpose, and is to be understood in relation to it. When Darwin proposed that man had evolved from lower forms of life there was an uproar. However, over time Christian apologists argued that God had created man by means of evolution, thus preserving the Judaeo-Christian view that all is to be explained in terms of God's foreordained purpose. The present, then, is to be explained in terms of the future. Such a schema is called in scientific discussion a teleological cause, contrasted with efficient causation.

Survival is the principal motivating evolutionary development in Darwin's schema: one species develops into another over geological time because those variations in offspring which survive best persevere whereas others fall by the wayside. But survival is not the same as heading towards a goal. *Homo sapiens* has emerged because the series of variations that differentiate us from the chimpanzee were those that survived best. Also, *Homo sapiens* is not the end-point of evolution – in another 200,000 years a new creature may have emerged. What brings about this present state of affairs is a *prior* event, the efficient cause.

In a world of efficient causes morality has no place. There is no intentionality in an efficient cause: I am driven by an event that has occurred; I am driven in the direction in which I went. The kernel of morality lies in choice – that I am a source of action. An efficient cause is a blind action that reverberates on other beings and excludes the idea that any bit of reality is the source of action. Once an individual has choice, and is therefore the source of action, teleology has been introduced. I act for a

84

purpose, and purpose is a teleological cause. There is no choice if we are driven by efficient causes alone.

Survival is the only course of the efficient cause. Choice means there is another option. If pleasure is linked to survival , then choice means there are reasons for acting other than survival. Freud worked within a schema of efficient causes. He did allow choice, but it was the choice of delayed gratification: a deferment of pleasure in the service of survival, or an ability to deflect an efficient cause.

The method of free association rests upon efficient causality in that the reason for one set of words rests on a previous set. The determining cause, however, is a prohibited wish, about which the subject feels bad, that is below the threshold of consciousness. Freud's very first discoveries of the mind therefore include the assumption of a morality: desires about which I feel bad, and therefore desires about which I feel good.

Freud's moral view is blended with the physicalist model, which is structured on efficient causes. The motivating factor in this model is one of homeostasis: tension builds within the organism, which seeks discharge in order to restore its former state. The efficient cause is the tension state, which is reduced through the incorporation of food, water or a sexual object. This theory of motivation underpins Freud's metapsychological papers. His moral theory is expressed in *The Interpretation of Dreams*, dreams being distorted expressions of wishes about which we feel bad, and which we refrain from knowing about.

A wish is something *I* have, which *I* institute; something which originates in *me*. Freud, however, did not clear up a contradiction: in his moral model the implication is that the ego is the source of the action which has to undergo repression; but in his homeostatic model, the source of action is in the biological substrate of the personality, and therefore an 'it' and not the ego.

How are we to overcome the clash between these two views? As we are intentional beings, are we not subjected to drives, and do instincts have no place? It is clear that we are both intentional beings and also subjected to drives. The confusion arises from the fact that drives offer an explanation at a level that is not of practical concern. Imagine I am with a friend looking at a crowd of people standing around a rectangular field. He asks me why the people are there, and I tell him because of the force of gravity, and were it not for this force they would be floating in space, and I continue to give a little exposition of the law of gravity. The explanation I have given is valid and is an answer to my friend's question. It is the necessary background without which no other things could happen. But it is not what he wants to know.

After leaving a session, a patient has a hunger pang and rushes to a shop and eats a bar of chocolate. The next day he asks his analyst why he had this hunger pang. The analyst explains that the organism requires energy to keep the system going, and food is this energy conveniently stored. He continues by explaining that when this energy has been used up a state of tension builds in the organism, and that this is experienced subjectively as hunger. The patient interrupts impatiently at this point and says he knows this already. The medical analyst then shakes himself out of his reverie, realizing he is not lecturing a medical student but is an analyst with a patient seeking the meaning of his hunger, and not the psychological model of hunger. He says to his patient that he believes that the revelation in the previous session about his death wishes towards himself made him eat the chocolate to try to assuage his anxiety. It is not that the first explanation is wrong, but that it has no meaning for the patient.

The drive theory operates at a different level, and has no explanatory power at the interpersonal and intrapsychic level. Why, then, was it held on to so tenaciously by Freud? I believe it was because he believed that if he abandoned this model he would be renouncing scientific explanation. I believe this is a misconception that has remained in psychoanalysis and continues to be harboured in all schools, though much more in some than in others. All I wish to emphasize here is that the drive theory does not have to be abandoned any more than the theory of gravity does, but that it is not relevant to the sphere of explanation we are investigating.

In *Three Essays on Sexuality*, Freud says that a drive has a source, an aim and an object. The source of the drive is in the biological substrate; the aim is the discharge of tension through one of the erotogenic zones; and the object is that through which the aim is satisfied. The sexual object is then the means to an end, where the end is the aim which is the reduction in the organism's state of tension. In this theory it is of no consequence what the object is that reduces the tension: whatever reduces the sexual drive, whether it be copulation between a man and woman, sexual encounter between man and man or woman and woman, or masturbatory fantasy, as long as it reduces the sexual drive it serves its purpose. Freud was in fact extremely interested in the different nature of these objects and theorized about them, but in terms of his theory they are not differentiated, and are not of consequence.

The object was invested with a stature of primary importance by many followers of Freud, especially Melanie Klein and Donald Winnicott. However, the only psychoanalyst who took the logical step of altering

Freud's theory was Ronald Fairbairn, who said that a drive was object-seeking in its nature, and so what had been an aim in Freud's theory became a means in Fairbairn's. Fairbairn said that the drive was object-seeking, and the erotogenic zone was the pathway along which it had to travel in order to reach its goal, and so it was a means to an end. What for Freud had been the end became the means, and what had been the means became the end. This led to a development which was of extreme importance in psychoanalytic practice: the way in which the object was treated became the focus of clinical work. In England this became known as the British School of Psychoanalysis or object relations, and its luminaries were Klein, Winnicott and Fairbairn.

These three had very different formulations as to the origins of pathology, but in one matter they agreed – that in the earliest stage of development the infant was focused entirely upon itself and its own pain, and it then progressed to a stage where it focused upon the other and its treatment of the other. This earliest stage was called the paranoid-schizoid position by Klein, the stage of ruthlessness by Winnicott and the schizoid position by Fairbairn. The stage at which the infant began to take notice of others and how it treated them was called the depressive position (Klein), the stage of concern (Winnicott) and the stage of object love (Fairbairn). Bad treatment of the other produces guilt which is intense and cannot be sustained and known. The ego projects its guilty acts into others, splits itself, and puts the bad parts of itself into outer objects. Its basic action is to shatter the self and project the different parts into outer objects, the body, or the future or past.

The psychology of these three psychoanalysts was based on the belief that the way the individual treated the other determined the individual's psychological state, and in repairing damage done to the object the psychological state of the self was also restored. The damaged object is the reality of the self and also the other.

While there are differences between these three theorists, they are unanimous in believing that psychological health depends on the capacity of the ego to achieve a good relation with the other, the object, and the reality of the self. This fundamental direction of the self towards the object is what we call the individual's emotional life. At this fundamental level the emotional life is coextensive with moral direction; in fact it means moral direction at a very basic level of functioning. In the British School we witnessed a shift from the sexual to the emotional, and the latter instead of the former became the focus of psychoanalytic investigation.

This change of focus from determinist science/efficient causation to a moral direction/teleological causation was a profound one. It was, I believe, the direction in which Freud was travelling but one that he was not fully able to take or acknowledge. His followers in the British School travelled further in that direction, but like Freud were not able to acknowledge that they had abandoned the model of efficient causation and had espoused a model which was moral.

It may be argued that this is a moral and not a religious view of the individual, but I believe this judgement to be made from the Judaeo-Christian perspective. The thesis upheld in this book is that the moral perspective *is* a religious one. The reason for defining it as moral and not religious is that the latter assumes the existence of God, which I believe to be an incorrect view because, on the one hand, belief in the existence of God is compatible with irreligion, and, on the other, the denial of God's existence is compatible with religion. My conclusion then is that the model of man embraced by the object relations school is a moral one. So, for instance, depression is caused by damage that has been done to the object.

This view was adumbrated by Freud, but as it contradicted the physicalist model it could not be explicitly stated. It was developed most fully theoretically by Fairbairn; it was also followed clinically by Klein and Winnicott, but both kept to Freud's homeostatic model theoretically.

Thus an important school of psychoanalysis has a spiritual aim in its clinical practice. It has influenced psychoanalysis in many parts of the world, but there is also considerable opposition to it from other schools. For example, I believe the enormous change in outlook that has occurred has not been recognized by either those analysts or academics who are interested in Freudian theory.

REFERENCE

Ilham Dilman (1984) *Freud and the Mind* (Oxford: Basil Blackwell), p. 3.

12

The Current Relation Between Psychoanalysis and Religion

Freud talks about the 'future of an illusion' as if he thought that religion itself was an illusion; it may be, but I think it is a basic illusion. Any particular religion changes with the prevalent fashion, but the fundamental thing, religion itself, does not.

(Bion, 1992)

Only a few psychoanalysts since Freud have directed their interest to religion. With some notable exceptions those few have confined themselves to the Judaeo-Christian religion. Some valuable work has been done in undoing the bias of Freud's *The Future of an Illusion*. In this work, as we have seen, Freud expressed the belief that the origin of religion lay in man's sense of helplessness in the face of the impersonal forces of nature. In order to fashion this implacable world into a more homely place, we invested these anarchic forces with human emotions so the mountains, streams, sunlight, and thunder became 'humanized'. If thunder was the anger of Zeus, it was comforting because we could then placate Zeus through sacrificial offerings and so exercise control. We were then no longer the helpless victims of fate.

Animism – that primitive stage of religion where spirits are attributed to the natural order – ceded to the pantheon of gods; then, through the rational workings of the mind, they gave way to a single god which satisfied our deep longing for a father who watches protectively over us. Religion is an illusion created to protect us from our feelings of infantile helplessness. As an illusory product, it is the universal neurosis of humankind that consumes psychic energy, and if released from this prison house, would be available for man's rational mastery of the world.

As we have seen, the first psychoanalyst to question this view was Freud's good friend, Oskar Pfister. Speaking from his deeply held faith, Pfister does not argue in a cogent way, but rather appeals to the emotions.

89

Pfister argues that civilization is a development and fulfilment of human nature rather than something that is antagonistic to our instincts, as Freud believed. To reduce humankind to drives and drive-derivatives is a reductionistic conceptualization which does not take account of desires, ideals and values. Pfister also believed that religion has been the seedbed of morality. Christian morality is based on the desires of the heart rather than on an external legal code: the Christian ideal of brotherly love is a realization of the desires of the heart, rather than an external demand that is in opposition to it. The command of God the Father is an expression of man's deepest yearning, therefore God as father is not born out of a desire to escape from infantile helplessness.

Pfister's account is not a scholarly critique of Freud's position, treading as he does the role of what might be called the sophisticated missionary (whereas the missionary of yesteryear tried to convert the infidel to his own point of view, the sophisticated missionary convinces himself that the infidel and himself at root believe the same).

Although the debate between Pfister and Freud is full of human interest, it is ultimately sterile: for all their humanity, they remain two dogmatists who shift not an inch from their credos. With one notable exception, all analysts interested in religion have harboured in their breasts both a Freud and a Pfister – but with no interchange between the two.

Gregory Zilboorg was born in 1890 in Russia of Jewish Orthodox parents. In 1919, just after the Bolshevik Revolution, Zilboorg emigrated to the United States where he soon gave up Judaism to become first a Quaker, and then towards the end of his life a Roman Catholic. He died in New York City in 1959.

Zilboorg had studied medicine, psychiatry, and psychoanalysis. He is, I suspect, with the exception of Meissner, the only psychoanalyst who had studied Thomas Aquinas and had a good grasp of his philosophy. I believe Zilboorg's most creative insight was to perceive that for both Freud and Aquinas the root of evil lay in a similar principle. For Freud it lay in the polymorphous infantile sexuality, whereas for Aquinas it lay in sensuality. Sensuality meant the indulgence of the sexual but, as Zilboorg points out, Aquinas understood this to include gluttony. Sensuality means the indulgence of pleasure. Of Freud, Zilboorg says, 'The conclusion which imposed itself upon Freud was that man cannot be considered grown-up or normal unless all the component infantile drives become fused into one genital constellation.'

90

In the infantile sexual state the individual is governed by the pleasures of each autonomous zone, whereas in maturity they are subordinated to the genital constellation. This means that they are governed by a purpose which is love. Freud states in his paper on narcissism that to begin to love is the basis for mental health. Creative love was also at the heart of Thomist morality. The source of evil, that which detracted man from his purpose, was the fixation on pleasure as a goal rather than as a secondary by-product of action. Thus Zilboorg argued that Freudian and Thomist morality has the same source and goal.

Zilboorg pointed out that Aquinas had recognized the truth in Aristotelian thinking and had incorporated it into his theology, although at the time Aristotle was considered a pagan and his teachings had been condemned by the Church only two decades before. In a similar way, Zilboorg believed that the Church should incorporate the psychological findings of the atheist Freud.

Zilboorg says that Freud's repudiation of religion was due to personal prejudice, and that his arguments against it are inconsistent with his arguments in regard to other human phenomena. For instance, Freud condemns man's attachment to the religious illusion, but is well disposed to the role of illusion in art; he accepts the sublimatory elements in the latter but not in the former. Therefore, Freud's arguments against religion are inconsistent.

However, Zilboorg is at fault in my view as he keeps Catholicism in one sphere and psychoanalysis in another. For instance, in his view confession is for the forgiveness of sin, whereas psychoanalysis is for the healing of neurosis and psychosis. There is no analysis of what is meant by sin, and no analysis of the factors that underlie neurosis and psychosis – he does not allow for the possibility that sin and neurosis or psychosis may have the same aetiology. I think the reason for this is that the sinful act is conscious whereas the psychic activities that give rise to neurosis and psychosis are unconscious. This is not to suppose, however, that the intentional act in both spheres may not be the same. Were Zilboorg to consider this it would mean questioning the value of some aspects of his Catholic practice, in particular the value of confession. He would also have to admit to the possibility that psychoanalysis has within it a moral dimension.

Zilboorg is committed to the view that psychoanalysis is a science, but he interprets science in a naturalistic sense. A methodology that is appropriate to our intentionality and interpersonal manner of communication is foreign to Zilboorg's conception of science. Psychoanalysis challenges religion to change its theology and practice, and religion in turn challenges the positivist scientific model that underlines much of Freud's psychoanalytic formulations. Zilboorg stops short of a mental revolution as great as this.

In a parallel fashion, Zilboorg says that *caritas* or *agape* – the sort of love that drove the saints and mystics – remains outside the field of psychological analysis. The roots of agape lie within the personality, and therefore are capable of psychological exploration. He is right in thinking that the deeper religious problems have hardly been touched by psychoanalysis, but this is not because they are not capable of being examined. I believe the reason Zilboorg takes this view is that he conceptualizes humankind according to Freud's structural model, and therefore bases the deepest drives in the impersonal id. On this basis the religious yearnings cannot be reached because the deepest source of human action lies in an option which is personal, and this model was not available to Zilboorg the analyst. The reason why psychoanalysts do not examine the personality using such a model, I believe, is because if they did they would discover that the religious category of faith, or its repudiation, is at the heart of the human endeavour. The analysts who do analyse on this assumption do not carry their practice through to its conceptual outcome.

Zilboorg does make connections between religion and psychoanalysis, perceptively drawing out certain common denominators, even if he does not allow any radical interpenetration between the two. Nevertheless, in the 1950s it took some courage to address the issue, and Zilboorg did not escape the vilification of Ernest Jones for his pains; the atheistic stance of Freud and some of his followers is invested with all the frenzy of the fanatic.

In more recent times, Stanley Leavy, a psychoanalyst and Christian, has written a book entitled *In the Image of God* (1988) as an *apologia* for Christianity, addressed presumably to his fellow analysts, psychotherapists and mental health professionals.

Leavy, a widely read man with an obvious love of history, looks at humans from an optimistic viewpoint. He is a Christian in the full sense of believing that God revealed himself in the life and teachings of Jesus Christ. The book is a personal meditation rather than a rigorous examination of the relations between psychoanalysis and Christianity. He draws parallels between the two, e.g., that psychoanalysis is the process of revealing what is hidden, and the events of Christ Jesus is the revealing of a hidden God. This kind of parallel creates a poetic imagery but has no real meaning; Zilboorg's discovery that Freud and Aquinas had a shared understanding of what underlay our sinfulness or waywardness is a true contribution to understanding.

Looking at psychoanalysis from a religious rather than a medical angle, Leavy's religious viewpoint has altered the prevailing positivistic model that underpins psychoanalysis:

> If we look on psychoanalysis as a deliberate, systematic attempt to understand the meaning of mental anguish in individuals and to relieve that anguish through the unconcealment of hidden intentions, we do not need to think in medical categories at all, or very little.

Although he discusses salvation from unhappiness and suffering, he does not consider the dissatisfaction from which patients seek relief within psychoanalysis. And like Zilboorg, Leavy talks of *nirvana* as 'the longings of a wearied people deprived of hope'. I point this out in order to highlight the fact that both analysts argue from a particular conviction which is narrow in its orbit. Leavy's book is less thorough than Zilboorg's, and it suffers from the same failure to question in a more radical way either the Christian religion or psychoanalysis. In both cases the psychoanalyst and the Christian are kept in compartments, although Zilboorg makes some illuminating connections between the origins of sin as understood by Aquinas, and the origins of neurosis and psychosis as understood by Freud.

Leavy's article 'Reality in Religion and Psychoanalysis' makes a plea for atheist analysts to be more tolerant towards patients who believe in God, stating clearly that to judge this belief of patients to be neurotic emanates from a prejudice. I shall take the opportunity here to examine briefly what is meant by God and the psychological nature of belief.

If I erect an image of a father-god as a defence against feelings of infantile helplessness and the fears that this generates, my analyst has the duty to help me develop into an adult. The psychoanalyst whose task it is to assist in this interior rite of passage will need to unmask the way in which this protective father-god has been erected in order to hide from me my infantile state and the emotional task which lies before me. If my belief in God is such an image, and under analysis this image dissolves, I may become an atheist. However, such a superficial change demonstrates that my theism was a sensual illusion rather than a judgement based upon knowledge.

There are therefore three possible conclusions: theism, agnosticism and atheism, all of which are arrived at through ontological reflection. If these are arrived at through a personal act of judgement, there will be tolerance of the point of view of others. However, I cannot tolerate the view of another if my own is the product of an identification with an idealized image. If I bury my infantile self in the aura of another's psychological attitude, I cannot tolerate something that challenges this because it threatens to reveal my own infantile dependence. I think that much fanaticism and intolerance finds its roots in this psychological fact.

In his article, Leavy develops and comments on the views of Hans Loewald, and there are three particular issues I wish to address. The first is his view that in the pre-Oedipal mother–child unit there is no opposition of reality to the developing ego. For a mother–child unit to be possible, father has to be shut out. If father stands for the true self or reality, the mother–child unit is very much in opposition to reality. This inner component has an outer correlative, which is the way the individual is perceived by others. A narcissistic patient is usually circumscribed within the boundaries of the mother–child unit: I do not see anything from the point of view of another, which would be to risk seeing myself as a baby with Mumma.

Leavy says that the heart of Loewald's revision of psychoanalytic theory lies in his conception of the process of internalization, which he sees as arising from the interactions within the mother–child unit. However, this is too vague to be of use, and he does not examine what particular action it is that leads to internalization. I think I only internalize when I *do* – no internalization takes place in the absence of this. Different actions of different parts of myself lead to multiple identifications. The reader may wish to reject my view of internalization, but he must replace it with another. Loewald's description is too general and does not pinpoint the factor that leads to internalization.

It would be possible to follow this through when Loewald comes to consider internalization from the Christian cultural perspective, but instead I want to point to what I believe is Leavy's mistaken view of the Resurrection. Leavy thinks that belief in the Resurrection of Christ came about as a result of Jesus having been seen by the Apostles in 'appearances' described in the Gospels. I believe that the core of this belief lay in an internal experience. A Christian's belief in the Resurrection lies in the fact that God the Father raised Christ from the dead, but for 'Christ' it must be understood that the whole of humankind is intended, which is now in a renovated state, having passed once again out of the bondage of Egypt and through the Red Sea, into a new Promised Land. This is the new Exodus, a new saving act of God. The Resurrection which lies at the heart of Christian doctrine was a mighty intervention by God towards his People, just as the Exodus had been of old. The bodily appearances of Jesus were faint manifestations of this saving act of God. The core of the Judaeo-Christian-Islamic belief is that the transcendent God bowed down towards the people and intervened in their history. In Judaism, this supreme moment – the *kairos* – occurred when Moses led his People out of Egypt; in Christianity when God raised Christ from the dead; in Islam when God revealed his Word to the Prophet. It would appear that Leavy has not conceptualized this clearly.

Although, as I have said, Leavy compartmentalizes religion and psychoanalysis and limits religion effectively to Christian belief, yet he does psychoanalysis a service by showing the prejudicial attitudes of analysts. He also writes in an attractive, appealing manner which will no doubt do a lot to banish the prejudices that he elucidates.

The Birth of the Living God by psychoanalyst Ana-Maria Rizzuto is a very interesting study of how the God representation is formed through an investment of parental imagos. This is a very valuable monograph on this aspect of religion. The author states specifically that her book is not a study of religion; however it is a detailed study of a very important component of most mature religions.

In his discussion of psychoanalysis in *Contemporary Psychoanalysis and Religion*, J. W. Jones focuses upon the transference, and demonstrates that the model of transference developed by the analysts of the British School rejects linear causality, which they have replaced with an interactional model. However, he does not recognize that the external interaction symbolizes inner structural relations; that what is done to the analyst in the transference is symbolical of what is being done to the reality of the self. In the structure of the self he does not seem to recognize that the principal active agents which are responsible for the mental condition of the individual are to be found within the inner psychic constellation.

Jones also equates religion with belief in God; his concept of God is cultic. His conceptualization of the self is in the Romantic tradition – a self that resonates with the *mysterium tremendum*, but the locus of this resonance is in ecstatic experience. It is a cultic outside God with whom the individual self has an ecstatic encounter, which occurs in the senses. For all the romanticizing language this is couched in, submission to an awe-filled God is the prime sign of *primitive* rather than *mature* religion. It is quite different from the reality-which-we-are which was known through contemplation by the seers of the Upanishads. In this case it is known through a mental act, whereas in the other it is known through an ecstatic experience.

The accent of this psychology is upon what has been done to the self, as opposed to how I live my life and how I construct my world. If I take my stand upon what blows of fate my own self has sustained, then I bow down to the *mysterium tremendum* and offer sacrifice instead of emotionally reconstructing my psychological world. Therefore, for all the valuable insights and synthesizing Jones offers, he tries ultimately to make a link between an analysis of adjustment and primitive mentality. We have already examined the latter; an analysis of social adjustment, as opposed to an analysis which is a cure of soul, will be discussed in the next chapter.

REFERENCES

Wilfred Bion (1992) *Cogitations* (London and New York: Karnac), p. 374.

Nina Coltart (1992) 'The Practice of Psychoanalysis and Buddhism' in *Slouching Towards Bethlehem . . .* (London: Free Association Press).

J. W. Jones (1991) *Contemporary Psychoanalysis and Religion* (New Haven and London: Yale University Press).

Stanley Leavy (1988) *In the Image of God* (New Haven and London: Yale University Press).

Hans Loewald (1978) 'Comments on Religious Experience' in *Psychoanalysis and the History of the Individual* (New Haven and London: Yale University Press).

W. W. Meissner (1984) *Psychoanalysis and Religious Experience* (New Haven and London: Yale University Press).

Ana-Maria Rizzuto (1979) *The Birth of the Living God* (Chicago and London: University of Chicago Press).

Antoine Vergote (1988) *Guilt and Desire* (New Haven and London: Yale University Press).

— (1990) 'Confrontation with Neutrality in Theory and Praxis' in *Psychoanalysis and Religion* (Baltimore and London: Johns Hopkins University Press), pp. 81–2.

Gregory Zilboorg (1967) *Psycho-analysis and Religion* (London: George Allen and Unwin).

13

Erich Fromm's Assessment of Religion

Love and do what you will.
(St Augustine)

I have stressed that all psychoanalysts writing on psychoanalysis and religion have kept the two disciplines in watertight compartments, not allowing either to penetrate or influence the other. The result of this has been that the author's religion remains unmodified by psychoanalysis, and vice versa. There is a polite dialogue, but there is no intention that their version of religion should alter one iota, and psychoanalysis must also not be affected in any radical way. The only person who stands out as an exception to this is Eric Fromm, and I have therefore devoted a whole chapter to his book *Psychoanalysis and Religion*. It is a very short book, but its value is in inverse ratio to its length.

Fromm begins by saying that although the modern world has developed an amazing technology which should greatly enhance our happiness, this has not been the case. That ancient ideal, 'the perfection of man' has not moved forward one inch; all this technology has done nothing to bring us closer to achieving our purpose in living.

In traditional religion, people go to church and listen to sermons in which the principles of love are preached – but the same people would not scruple to sell a commodity which they knew a customer could not afford. I put the following question once to a priest: A customer comes into a bookshop and is about to buy a hardback copy of *Oliver Twist*. As he hands it to the bookseller, he mentions that it is expensive. The bookseller knows he has a much cheaper paperback copy. Does the bookseller have an obligation to tell the customer that there is a cheaper edition? The priest answered he had not, yet does not the gospel of love dictate that he let his neighbour know there is a cheaper edition available in the shop? There is an easy test which elucidates the answer. If you went into a bookshop and had a similar experience, but as you were about to pay for the book the bookseller told you there was also a cheaper edition available, what would your opinion of him be? That he was a decent man? That he gained your respect? If he did *not* do this you would say he was within his rights, but he would not command the higher sentiments of respect and gratitude.

This is an example much in the spirit of what Fromm is concerned with. There are many who would consider the bookseller who informed his customer to be a fool. Fromm's reply is that the Western world has become enslaved to anti-human values; the human has been judged subservient to a new idolatry: money-making, success, power, and domination over others. The modern world, then, is faced with a huge problem: although there is a marvellous technology at our disposal, and thus the wherewithal to extend greatly the range of our well-being, yet it is used to a great extent to enslave human beings to things. It is a new idolatry.

Academic psychology has no interest in the soul and in virtue, but instead apes the natural sciences and so only concentrates upon those elements which can be counted and measured. Concepts like conscience, value judgements and the knowledge of good and evil are banished and put into the category of metaphysics. The concern for the human soul has been left to the philosophers. Fromm implies that the problems of most pressing psychological moment have remained the province of philosophy.

Fromm also complains that priests and ministers of religion are the only professional groups who are recognized as being concerned with the soul, the only spokespeople for the ideals of love, truth and justice, whereas in ancient Greece it was also the province of philosophers like Socrates, Plato and Aristotle, who did not speak in the name of revelation, but with the authority of reason.

In comparing Freud's and Jung's attitude to religion, Fromm says that the core values of the great religions are the pursuit of truth, of freedom, and of brotherly love, and that these values were central for Buddhism, Christianity and Hinduism. He is concerned with what is the true end of humankind, which he stresses is the achievement of personal responsibility. In order to achieve this personal responsibility, the individual has to free himself from the need of a protective father. Fromm says that it is precisely this that Freud advocates in *The Future of an Illusion*, and argues that Freud therefore promotes precisely those values that are central to religion. In terms of the distinction which I have made in this book, Fromm is arguing that Freud supports with vigour those core values which are mediated by mature religion, although he leaves out of the discussion whether Freud had any realization of this.

Erich Fromm's assessment of religion

That Freud was so fanatically atheistic and such an outspoken opponent of religion does not bother Fromm because he believes that it is in action that an individual demonstrates his religious adherence rather than in words: '. . . some of the most ardent "atheists", devoting their lives to the betterment of mankind, to deeds of brotherliness and love, have exhibited faith and a profoundly religious attitude.' Fromm thought that Freud was rejecting precisely those attitudes, enshrined in much of the paraphernalia of traditional religion, that hamper men and women from achieving personal responsibility.

For Fromm, Freud's attitude to religion is much more congenial than Jung's. His main critique of Jung is that he enshrines submission to authority as the core religious attitude, which for Fromm is anathema. Fromm makes a distinction between two different attitudes which permeate religious experience: the authoritarian and the humanitarian. The former embodies submission to authority as an escape from inner feelings of loneliness and limitation. One could add that people also take flight from knowledge of their own greed, envy, sadism and hatred into a submission of this kind. The pay-off from psychological submission is ignorance of one's own evil doings.

Religious hypocrisy such as one sees in a character like Tartuffe, or in Prince Luzhin in *Crime and Punishment*, masquerades always under the kind of submission to authority that Fromm describes. (It is worth noting that many a patient erects the psychoanalyst into an authoritarian god, to whom he subtly submits precisely to hide from view his own falseness, envy, hostility and destructiveness.) Fromm believes that Jung supports religion of this authoritarian kind and therefore his approach is inimical to the development of the responsibility and personal freedom which is the *sine qua non* of being a human being, and is the foundation stone of all genuine religion. Fromm also criticizes Jung for the same reasons as I have done in my chapter on Jung. He deplores Jung's definition of objectivity as the *consentium gentium*, and points out how often in recent history we have been witnesses to a *folie à millions*.

For Fromm, in order to become a responsible human being with the capacity to love and with the ability to seek the truth it is necessary to become free of incestuous ties. The sexual instinct is not the core of the matter as Freud insisted, but rather that incest is a state in which the individual is emotionally stuck, deriving consoling feelings by remaining a child requiring a protective authority. The person may enjoy a kind of animal affection, like living in a warm womb, but there is a big price to be paid for it. He does not develop the capacity to make his own choices; he needs to be loved but does not have the capacity to love. Initially, this need is for the warm, consoling protection from his mother and father and family, but this can spread out to a wider grouping, such as a tribe, a nation or a religious denomination.

It is for this reason that Kleinian analysts concentrate their attention on the infantile transference – those psychological attitudes deriving from childhood that are still active in the way the person relates to himself and his fellows. The analyst's aim is to transform childlike attitudes into adult emotions. In this way, Fromm sees psychoanalysis as religion's handmaid rather than its opponent. This statement, though, needs some qualification.

Just as Fromm distinguishes between authoritarian and humanistic religion, so also he distinguishes between a psychoanalysis which aims at social adjustment and that which aims at the cure of soul. He points out in a footnote that the word 'cure' is a transliteration of the Latin *cura*, which means the care of, rather than the medical idea of remedial treatment. Some psychoanalysts aim at social adjustment whereas others aim at cure of the soul. I quote here in part a case which Fromm uses to illustrate the distinction:

> A young man of twenty-four comes to see an analyst; he reports that since his graduation from college two years ago he has felt miserable . . . . He was very interested in physics; his teacher had told him that he had considerable gifts for theoretical physics and he had wanted to go to graduate school and find his life's work as a scientist. His father, a well-to-do businessman, owner of a large factory, insisted that the son should enter the business. . . . as a result of his father's promises, warnings, and appeals to his sense of loyalty, [the son] had given in and entered his father's firm. Then the troubles described above began . . .
>
> If one is prone to believe that 'adjustment' to the social patterns is the paramount aim of life, that practical considerations like the continuity of a firm, higher income, gratitude toward parents are prime considerations, one will also be more inclined to interpret the son's trouble in terms of his irrational antagonism to the father. If, on the other hand, one considers integrity, independence, and the doing of work meaningful to the person as supreme values, one will be prone to look at the son's inability to assert himself and his fear of his father as the main difficulties to be resolved.

Just as Fromm is critical of authoritarian religion, so he is also critical of the type of psychoanalysis that aims at social adjustment. Fromm is therefore promoting a particular value which is found both in religion and in psychoanalysis. As a description of religion he calls it 'humanitarian', and in psychoanalysis 'cure of souls'. As the two attitudes are the same, for the sake of clarity it would help if Fromm had a single name to cover both. The one that comes most readily to mind is 'responsible freedom', the supreme value for Fromm, and the core value in both mature religion and psychoanalysis. Responsible freedom is the opposite of freedom to do whatever you want, for which the proper word is licence. Responsible freedom means freedom to do the good; it recognizes that there is such a value as 'the good' and that stunted emotional development impedes its realization.

Just as Fromm does not carry through his conceptualizations to a unified understanding, so also he does not make clear the detachment necessary for responsible freedom to become established. However, this supreme value unifies the aims of psychoanalysis and mature religion: the two do not inhabit separate compartments but rather are integrated through finding the value which synthesizes the two. For this reason, I believe Fromm has a deeper understanding of psychoanalysis and religion than any other analytic writer.

I have two criticisms to make of Fromm's approach, one of which I have already touched upon. First, his criticism of Jung is fully justified, but his adulation of Freud is exaggerated. His interpretation of Freud was not Freud's own, and Fromm's position would have been more convincing if he had made this point. It is clearly right that responsible freedom is a value which Freud expresses clearly in *The Future of an Illusion*, but to give the impression that Freud therefore was supportive of religion would require considerable explanation. We require of Fromm some acknowledgement of Freud's implacable hostility to religion. If Fromm had said that Freud had done humanitarian religion a service through elucidating a path along which people are able to obtain responsible freedom we would have no quarrel, but he seems to leave out of his account Freud's manifest antagonism.

The second criticism is a more serious one. It is Fromm's making external what are often internal difficulties, a tendency that emerges clearly in the case quoted above. Fromm makes it look as if the conflict is between the boy and his father, whereas in fact the emotional struggle is between a part of the boy that wants to study physics, and another that wants what his father wants. To spell the matter out conceptually, there is a struggle taking place between a true inner sense of value and a value that is not true to him. The latter is seductive because it is better paid and gives him more authoritarian power. It is a struggle between God and the devil, good and bad, or the true and the false as components of the soul. Fromm does not draw out the elemental battle that rages within, and yet this is the core of all spiritual endeavour. Therefore, despite all its insightful accuracy, the religious values which Fromm advocates are external and devoid of spirituality. So, for instance, he stresses the consumerism of capitalist society and makes the enemy of religion an external one, whereas the founders of mature religion have all taught that the enemy is within; our fundamental battle is an inner one. The Buddha's battle was with Mara and the battle that Jesus fought was with the devil within and so also with the prophet Jeremiah.

This lacuna in Fromm's thinking is reflected in his definition of religion: 'Any system of thought and action shared by a group which gives the individual a frame of orientation and an object of devotion.' Yet such a definition could fit Communism or Nazism. The central spiritual task is detachment, and it is clear from later writings (for example, *For the Love of Life*) that detachment is a personal ideal for Fromm, but it has not been incorporated into his definition of religion. The definition and approach to religion is one of humanitarian social action; elevated though this is it lacks spirituality, without which religion ceases to be a religion.

Despite these criticisms, which are important in the extreme, Fromm has, I believe, integrated religion and psychoanalysis more successfully than any analytic thinker before or after him, and I have followed this aspect of his general approach in this book.

REFERENCES

Sigmund Freud (1927) *The Future of an Illusion*, SE, vol. XXI.
Erich Fromm (1972) *Psychoanalysis and Religion* (United States and Canada: Bantam Books).
— (1983) *For the Love of Life* (New York: The Free Press).

PART THREE

Throughout this book I have used the term 'mature' for the new form of religion that first arose in the Axial Era. Sociologists, anthropologists and those who have made religion a topic of scientific study have named this same religious form 'salvationist' or 'liberationist'. Such terms describe a goal shared by all of these religions: the desire in human beings to be liberated from the situation in which they find themselves.

These great teachers of the Axial Era came forward in response to something. Even in the mythology of primitive religion human beings already felt there was something wrong, something amiss. The biblical story of the Fall is familiar to most people, and we have referred to a similar legend in Dinka mythology. In all the myths there is the message that the state in which human beings find themselves was brought about through disobedience to a fundamental command which was understood and known in the culture: they themselves, therefore, had done something that brought about this pitiable state. In this, however, there also lay hope: if it was within human capability to bring disaster upon himself, then it was also within his grasp to start repairing what he had brought about.

I attempt in this section to examine the state in which we find ourselves. It is my belief that this state can only be changed by a regeneration which comes from within, and that the enormous scientific achievements especially of the last two centuries have done nothing to improve the state of humankind which the mythology of primitive religion set about to describe. Therefore there is still an inner task for us. We are born into a world which we are challenged to change, but the place that requires the most urgent attention is within ourselves.

14

The Human Condition

'Did you say the stars were worlds, Tess?'
'Yes.'
'All like ours?'
'I don't know; but I think so . . . Most of them are splendid and sound – a few blighted.'
'Which do we live on – a splendid or blighted one?'
'A blighted one.'
"Tis very unlucky that we didn't pitch on a sound one, when there were so many more of
'em!'

(Hardy, 1984)

The message of those great masters of spiritual living, the masters who arose in the Axial and post-Axial Eras, was that the human purpose is not to survive bodily at all costs. To offer sacrifice may bring rain, may bring a richer harvest, but there is more to life than this – there is an inwardness, the fulfilment of which gives life its purpose. Attention to this inner life and its development brings a serenity that surpasses the more transitory pleasures of existence. The fruit of attentiveness to our inner life is compassion for our fellow human beings, for all living things, and for our world. This was the message of the masters: cultivate the good, attend to what is inner, and have compassion for your fellow man and woman. It was a message which was spoken with disarming simplicity; to achieve the goal they put before their followers, however, was a task of supreme difficulty.

What these spiritual teachers set forth was a path. To be true to one's inmost self and to live accordingly and act with compassion was the path to be followed, but they did not put forward a prescription as to how to live. They did something more profound in that they showed that to live according to the guidelines they laid down fulfilled our potential but, as St Paul says:

In my inmost self I dearly love God's Law, but I can see that my body follows a different law that battles against the law which my reason dictates. This is what makes me a prisoner of that law of sin which lives inside my body.

(Romans 7:22–23)

105

There is some principle, a 'different law', that battles against our reason. This can be seen clearly in the Platonic dialogues where Socrates has to battle point by point against enormous emotional pressure to accept what is against reason. The Buddha also had an enormous struggle against Mara, the principle of Evil, before he attained Enlightenment:

> Mara uttered fear-inspiring threats and raised a whirlwind so that the skies were darkened and the ocean roared and trembled. But the Blessed One under the Bodhi-tree remained calm and feared not.
>
> (Carus, 1990)

When Jesus decided to go to Jerusalem and face his destiny, Peter attempted to dissuade him. This is the record of it in the Gospel of Matthew (16:24–28):

> From that time Jesus began to make it clear to his disciples that he was destined to go to Jerusalem and suffer grievously at the hands of the elders and chief priests and scribes, to be put to death and to be raised up on the third day. Then, taking him aside, Peter started to remonstrate with him, 'Heaven preserve you, Lord;' he said 'this must not happen to you'. But he turned and said to Peter, 'Get behind me Satan! You are an obstacle in my path, because the way you think is not God's way but man's.'

This last passage illustrates the way in which the individual can be tempted away from the right path even by the counsel of a close friend, which can be inspired by Satan or the Evil One.

We have here, then, in two entirely different traditions the same message: a powerful force exists that seduces us away from the path of truth. In Buddhist teaching this evil works its wicked way through ignorance; it is through blindness that the individual does things that are contrary to the true path. Thus we are all immersed in a situation which blinds us to the true path, which will bring us fulfilment. The blindness is due to our eyes being focused upon external, rather than internal, events.

Before the Axial Era humans lived in a primitive state bound by instinct to the signals of survival. They were ignorant of the potential within them that was capable of lifting them to a new level of awareness. The arrival of the great spiritual masters was thus like a beacon of light shining in a darkness which had never been pierced before.

In Christian doctrine, this condition in which the human is set against his best interests was attributed to the sin of Adam, and has been called the Fall of Man by Christian theologians. In the Christian view, this plunged the whole human race into a state of raw ungodliness. This state is well described by Cardinal Newman (1962):

> To consider the world in its length and breadth, its various history, the many races of man, their fortunes, their mutual alienation, their conflicts; and then their ways, habits, governments, forms of worship; their enterprises, their aimless courses, their random achievements and acquirements, the impotent conclusion of long-standing facts, the tokens so faint and broken, of a superintending design, the blind evolution of what turn out to be great powers or truths, the progress of things, as if from unreasoning elements, not towards final causes, the greatness and littleness of man, his far-reaching aims, his short duration, the curtain hung over his futurity, the disappointments of life, the defeat of good, the success of evil, physical pain, mental anguish, the prevalence and intensity of sin, the pervading idolatries, the corruptions, the dreary hopeless irreligion, that condition of the whole race, so fearfully yet exactly described in the Apostle's words, 'having no hope and without God in the world,' – all this is a vision to dizzy and appal; and inflicts upon the mind the sense of a profound mystery, which is absolutely beyond human solution.
>
> What shall be said to this heart-piercing, reason-bewildering fact? I can only answer, that either there is no Creator, or this living society of man is in a true sense discarded from His presence. Did I see a boy of good make and mind, with the tokens on him of a refined nature, cast upon the world without provision, unable to say whence he came, his birthplace or his family connections, I should conclude that there was some mystery connected with his history, and that he was one, of whom, from one cause or other, his parents were ashamed. Thus only should I be able to account for the contrast between the promise and condition of his being. And so I argue about the world; – *if* there be a God, *since* there is a God, the human race is implicated in some terrible aboriginal calamity.

When Newman offers the simile of a boy 'with the tokens on him of a refined nature' the inference is that man lived at some higher level and fell on evil days. This is not the interpretation that is being offered here.

That the human scene is rent with disaster and catastrophe on all sides only the blind could deny. We have only to give one sweeping look around our everyday world to behold horrors from which all must shrink in horror. The day this is being written we are hit by news headlines of another appalling massacre in South Africa. A peaceful demonstration marching towards the border of Ciskei keeping faithfully to the permitted guidelines for the demonstration is suddenly shattered with gunfire from a vengeful police force and 28 people are killed and over 200 are wounded. Only three months before there had been another such massacre at Boipotong. In the same news bulletins comes the news of multiple deaths in Somalia, and daily innocent people are shelled to death in Sarajevo. In 1989 in El Salvador six Jesuits were brutally murdered for trying to uphold human rights under a psychopathic dictatorship. In China in 1989 thousands of demonstrators were brutally murdered in Tiananmen Square. A girl of twelve was riding innocently on her bicycle when a truck with soldiers passed her and they shot her down in their orgy of killing. The government in Guatemala is trying to promote tourism and thinks that the sight of street children will deter tourists from coming, so the police have been rounding up the children and shooting them.

The following report by Arvind N. Das of New Delhi came from *The Times of India* on 15 January 1992:

> It has been alleged that the Central Jalma Institute for Leprosy in Agra, a permanent institute of the Indian Council for Medical Research, lures leprosy patients to be admitted for treatment and then fraudulently removes their organs like kidneys and eyes for sale to rich persons who need such organs for transplant . . .
>
> Once they arrive in Agra where they are unfamiliar with the local language, they are admitted to the institute, given some treatment and then an attempt is made to convince them it is necessary to remove some of their organs in order to prevent the spread of leprosy in their bodies . . .

We only have to travel back fifty years in our own century to the appalling massacre of Jews by the Nazis in Germany with a technical brutality not equalled in the annals of history and through such a foul butchery six millions perished entirely. Twenty-five years earlier the Turks massacred well nigh a million Armenians. Human savagery goes back over the centuries and over the millennia to the dawning of civilization.

Sometimes the words 'animal', 'bestial' or 'brutal' are applied to the behaviour of human beings, but often the behaviour is far worse than anything recorded in the lower levels of the animal kingdom. Some animals are predators that kill other animals for their food, but it is always in the service of survival.

I have made the point that when humans began to bury their dead it was an evolutionary step, culminating some 60,000 years later in the emergence of mature religion in the Axial Era. With this step, however, there also came an enormous intensification of the potential for good and for evil. Good and evil only arise when the object has individual value. If I strike an object with a stick and someone tells me, 'That object was an empty Coca-Cola can', then my act of striking is neither good nor bad. It is morally neutral. However, if I am told, 'You have just struck a baby, which is now in pain', the potential for good or bad immediately arises. When humans started to bury their dead it signified a new object, or new awareness of the object which is the same – an object judged to have value.

The primordial struggle between good and evil that characterized this new era in human development was symbolized in the struggle that occurred within the great spiritual masters, which has continued through religious history in the lives of mystics. The new potential which emerged from a servile bondage was a capability for extreme wickedness and heroic goodness. It was a capability that humankind had not had before then, like atomic power, which could be used for extreme good or extreme bad.

It is frequently said of the monsters of history that they might so easily have been powers for extreme good. While some traumas can easily tempt a person to pursue evil, they can also be the opportunity for sanctity. At the end of the First World War, Hitler was blinded and lay helpless in hospital as the German nation surrendered. Churchill (1948) says of him:

> The shock of defeat, the collapse of law and order, the triumph of the French, caused this convalescent regimental orderly an agony which consumed his being, and generated those portentous and measureless forces of the spirit which may spell the rescue or the doom of mankind.

That is the story of one man who lay in a hospital bed and its calamitous outcome. There is another story of a soldier who lay in bed wounded, the story of Ignatius of Loyola. Again an agony consumed his being but on this occasion it turned him in the opposite direction. These are the words of his poet biographer, Francis Thompson (1962):

> The delight of these imaginings left him agitated and unblessed; while the diviner reverie left comfort behind. He noted the contrast, and it opened his understanding to the great test which proves whether communication and emotion be heavenly or unheavenly. Introspection

set in upon him; the example of the Saints more and more engrossed him; he began to account his life misspent; and with divine enlightenment came the resolve to imitate the Saints indeed.

The myth of Paradise represents the constant temptation that afflicts all of us to go to one side or the other; it is the permanent status of the human race. These 'measureless forces of the spirit' began their slow release with the emergence of primitive religion, and reached their historical climax in the Axial Era. Hitler murdered six million Jews for reasons of the spirit just as Mother Teresa nurses the poor and sick in Calcutta for reasons of the spirit. In each case it is the 'measureless forces of the spirit' – but with how different an intent, and how different an outcome.

We have in each of us this struggle between a Hitler and a Mother Teresa. We are always prone to take the path of Hitler, of the devil, of Mara, of the Evil One. What is this condition in which we all find ourselves? What is it that we need to be rescued from? The intent of the great teachers of the Axial and post-Axial Eras was to help us to rescue ourselves from this condition.

All these teachers have one message in common: life's meaning is to be found in a reality beyond the immediate, beyond the senses. This reality transcends survival, and therefore the instincts which drive us towards survival. If we pursue that which is pleasurable and avoid what is painful we are in bondage to an earthbound force, with our eyes fixed upon our own survival and comfort. Prior to the burial climax the survival instinct was group-bound; subsequently it individuated, and each person became tied to his own hedonistic impulses, caught within the circle of his own needs. The preoccupation of the individual was with opportunities for his own advantage; he was on the lookout for that which would satisfy, always fearful of danger, seeking pleasure and avoiding pain.

This is a state in which I am preoccupied with my own self-protection, my own favour with the elders of the tribe. Nothing higher suggests itself, no inner prompting to self-reflection asserts itself strongly enough to lift me out of the narrow boundaries of my prison. I am enclosed in myself and all purpose. The god who must be served above all else is myself – there is no other, no principle within or without, whether it be transcendent or immanent, that can raise me out of myself. This is the human condition – the state of affairs the prophet Amos railed against, that Socrates combated with all the force he could muster, that the Buddha spent his life in exhaustive work to overcome.

The human condition is also the source of all evil, wrongdoing, sin, suffering and human misery with which the world is so plentifully endowed. Could we not slip back to before the Axial Era? If the spirit is such a dangerous weapon to have at our disposal, would it not be better to return to our state of near animalhood? The Axial Era, with its teachers and prophets, was a challenge. Once humans had heard it they were in a new state; the spirit was awoken and there was no return. The person now had to go the way of Hitler or Loyola, Buddha or Genghis Khan: 'He who is not with me is against me' (Matthew 12:30). There is no turning back; we cannot return to that pre-spiritual state any more than we can return to our erstwhile primate existence. Given this state, we have a radical choice to make. Most of us hover in the middle – we do not reach the heroic heights of a Mother Teresa or the degrading depths of Hitler. Yet we are confronted with the choice every day.

We have used the words 'evil' and 'good', but in what do these categories consist? We all have within us a categorization of good and evil: it is wrong to murder; it is good to feed the hungry; it is wrong to steal; it is good to be generous; it is wrong to despise and so on. Another very important category to which right and wrong apply is the individual's relationship to his or her self. This is the sphere of conscience; it is also the sphere of psychoanalysis.

The sphere of good and evil applies in many channels of human communication that have no law. The moral law, such as the Decalogue, only describes very general principles and they are all external, identifiable actions. In the book *Black Like Me* by Howard Griffin, the author, a white, through dye and medicine makes himself black and travels around the southern states of America. He is shocked by the behaviour to which he is subjected by whites. What he finds particularly upsetting is the 'hate stare', for example, travelling on a bus a white would stare at him with contempt and hatred. There is no law against this; no moral authority can legislate against it, and yet such behaviour is a source of great perturbation in the human community.

We need inside us then a sense of what is right. What is wrong about the 'hate stare'? What is wrong with killing someone? There is some primordial sense within us that we are owed respect from our fellow humans, that others have this claim upon us, and that we have to live in such a way in order to rightfully claim such a respect. This requires that we live according to such a level; there is a primordial claim that I live according to this level, and such is our belief that we have the capacities in us to answer that claim.

'My life is my own. I don't owe anyone anything. I can kill myself if I like. Why shouldn't I steal if I want to, and commit adultery? No one has ever given me anything. Why shouldn't I take drugs? I am a free man after all. If I want to destroy myself, that's my funeral and it's no one else's business.'

What is at fault with this argument? Where is the fatal flaw? I am born with an expectation – something is expected of me, and this expectation is of myself. That my human nature is an object to be achieved and is not a given is the message which is at the very heart of mature religion. It is what was preached by Jesus, it was argued by Socrates, and it was at the centre of the Buddha's teaching. There is an object to be achieved. Many will aim at it but constantly fail, be torn away from their objective, but the extremity of evil consists in a dire refusal, which is probably what Jesus meant when he said, 'And so I tell you, every one of men's sins and blasphemies will be forgiven, but blasphemy against the Spirit will not be forgiven' (Matthew 12:31). To refuse the religious message which says that to be human is something to be achieved plunges the person into a spiritual anti-humanness which degrades a human being to a status less than the beasts. Jesus said,

> The Son of Man is going to his fate, as the scriptures say he will, but alas for that man by whom the Son of Man is betrayed! Better for that man if he had never been born!
>
> (Matthew 26:24)

The human condition to which all great religious leaders have addressed themselves is that we are in a position of unavoidable choice, a spiritual condition. The great religious teachers and the saints and mystics through the ages have understood deeply that the human condition is man's estate. They understood it through having encountered it in the extremity of their own being. This choice starts as an external one but then progresses to an inner one we have seen clearly in the life of the Buddha.

These teachers believed that the secret of life, what ultimately yielded meaning, was to choose that object through which we become most truly human. This object is real but does not have a material existence; its reality only comes into being in the act of being chosen. It is a mental object that cannot be shown through the senses; it has to be grasped intuitively through doing. When Jesus is asked, 'And who is my neighbour?', the only thing he can do is to tell a story and let those who can grasp it, grasp it, and so the Good Samaritan stands as an eternal parable in Western culture. In a similar way when a distressed woman came to the Buddha because one of her children had died he conveyed a truth to her through a dramatized parable. I quote again the story (Morgan, 1986):

> Kisa Gotami lost her only child and became almost mad with grief, not allowing anyone to take away her dead child in the hope that it might revive again through some miracle. She wandered everywhere and at last came into the presence of the Buddha. Buddha understood the deep sorrow that so blinded the poor mother, so after giving her comfort he told her that he could revive the child if she could procure a handful of mustard seeds from the house of one where no death had ever taken place. Hope came to her and she set forth from house to house asking for a handful of seeds. She did receive, everywhere, the seeds with profuse sympathy. But when it came to asking whether there had been any death in the family, everybody universally lamented the loss of a mother or a father or a son or daughter, and so on. She spent hours travelling in search of the precious seeds that promised the revival of her son, but alas, none could give them to her.
>
> A vision arose before her and she understood the implication of the Buddha's hint. She understood that death is inherent in life which is the source of all suffering and delusion.

The object has to be understood. This object then, this spiritual objective for human fulfilment, is pointed to constantly and through this form of teaching there is the possibility of a slow discernment of the true human objective. It is only understood through being personally grasped.

All truly spiritual persons have been aware of how easy it is to mistake the false object for the real one. This ignorance, this blindness to the truth, is also part of the human condition. It has ever been the role of the spiritual leader to conquer ignorance, to open our eyes to those things which we cannot see. It was one of Socrates's principles that you cannot do evil and see it at the same time, and the reverse is also true: you can only refuse life's objective if at the same time you blind yourself to your own actions. This particular matter will confront us even more forcefully when we consider the objective of psychoanalysis.

What I call mature religion includes those religious leaders and spiritual masters who have founded religions or movements, and have come to free man from a condition in which he lives and has his being it is an essential aspect of this human condition that he is both blind to the nature of his being and more intimately unknowing of what he does, and mature religion aims to save man from his ignorance. Similarly, shining a

light into the areas of a person's being that he does not know is the
primordial task of psychoanalysis; its prime task is to dispel ignorance. It is
for this reason that I believe that psychoanalysis has a spiritual function. In
the spiritual endeavour, the psychoanalyst attempts to see what we do, to
discern the true from the false, to differentiate good from evil.

REFERENCES

Paul Carus (1984) *The Gospel of Buddha* (Illinois: Open Court Press).
Winston Churchill (1948) *The Second World War: The Gathering Storm* (London:
    Cassell & Co.), vol. 1, p. 41.
John Howard Griffin (1966) *Black Like Me* (London: Collins), p. 65.
Thomas Hardy (1984) *Tess of the D'Urbervilles* (Harmondsworth: Penguin).
K. W. Morgan (1986) *The Path of the Buddha* (Delhi: Motilal Banarsidass).
John Henry Newman (1962) *Apologia Pro Vita Sua* (London: Fontana Books).
Francis Thompson (1962) *Saint Ignatius Loyola* (London: Burns & Oates/Universe
    Books), p. 7.

15

Narcissism and the Human Condition

Egoism consists in this: absolute opposition, an impassable gulf is fixed between one's own self and other beings. I am everything to myself and must be everything to others, but others are nothing in themselves and become something only as a means for me. My life and welfare is an end in itself, the life and welfare of others are only a means for my ends, the necessary environment for my self-assertion. I am the centre and the world only a circumference.

(Soloviev, 1918)

In the development of object relations theory, psychoanalysis changed from being a natural science into an ethical signifier in the sphere of emotional relations. Winnicott said that when the child is born he is in a stage of ruthlessness, and that in favourable circumstances this changes into the stage of concern. Many an adult, said Winnicott, is emotionally deficient and still stuck at the stage of ruthlessness, and it became a goal of treatment to assist such a patient into the stage of concern. Similarly, Melanie Klein had the view that the infant is born into the paranoid-schizoid stage of emotional development and an adult may become fixed at this stage of emotional development, unable to progress to what she named the depressive position.

Both Winnicott and Klein made the inference from their clinical observations that the infant starts life in a self-preoccupied state, unconcerned about the other, and progresses to a stage where the presence of the other begins to feature in its emotional world. As it was also the aim of both analysts to lead their patients to the second stage, they both made a value judgement that achievement of the second stage was a prerequisite for mental health. This value judgement also endorsed a basic moral perspective in psychoanalysis. The stage of ruthlessness or the paranoid-schizoid position is the human condition as encountered by psychoanalysts in their consulting-rooms. It is the human condition in the microsocial environment and in the emotional environment. Psychoanalysis aims to lead the patient out of this situation. The relationship between psycho-analysis and religion hinges on this.

It is necessary to recapitulate here the distinction which Erich Fromm makes between psychoanalysis which aims at social adjustment and psychoanalysis which aims at the cure of souls. An analysis which aims at the former does nothing to rescue individuals from the human condition. Such a treatment aims to adapt them externally to their living situation, and does not aim at restructuring the personality. In such an analysis, the analyst listens to the patient with sympathetic understanding, and through identifying sensitively with the patient's suffering gives him the feeling of being understood and not being alone in the world. In this mode the analyst sympathizes understandingly with the patient, with those things that have happened to the patient. There is, however, a flaw in this which I shall try to illustrate by telling you of a patient I once treated.

A man in his mid-forties, as he came through the door he greeted me cheerily. Although he had many talents, he had never persevered sufficiently in any one of them to have capitalized on his undoubted capabilities. So here he was, only moderately successful, with a foot in several camps; very entertaining at parties but with a marriage that was crumbling. He had a younger brother, Tony, who had contracted polio as a baby and had been left severely paralysed. Tony received all the attention from his mother, and so my patient felt obliged to present himself as having no problems in order to make things as easy for his mother as possible. He presented himself to me in the same way, and I interpreted to him that he felt all my attention was on my previous patient, who was Tony in his mind. He constantly thought that I was preoccupied with other patients, or with my family, and so on, all of which I related to his feeling that his mother's attention was on Tony. This was the kernel around which many interpretations were focused for the first nine months or so. By the end of a year he gave evidence of being a good deal better, but there were certain worrying things. He continued to hate his mother, and continued to be cruel to his brother. There was also a general sense of his being very self-centred.

In all this my patient felt supported: he had found someone who sympathized with him in his neglect, but there was always the sense that it was support from me *against* a life which had been unfair to him. This led me to wonder whether there was any true strength within my patient which was capable of changing his surroundings. Did it mean that his soul remained the same? With these questions rapping insistently at the door of my mind, he came in for a session, saying he was feeling fine. Soon, however, some discordant facts came trickling through. He had had a row with his girlfriend (he had separated from his wife); he had received a letter from his wife's solicitor claiming a sum in alimony which would cripple him financially. I remarked on the way he felt the need to declare that he was feeling fine when the truth was that disturbing happenings were bombarding him. Again he was playing out the role of little Michael telling his mummy-analyst that he was quite all right and had no problems. There was a touching pathos of the little boy feeling he needed to keep all these painful things inside him and not share them. I might have left things with the gentle understanding that existed between us undisturbed, but a hard question confronted me: why did he play out this role with me? Why did he pretend to have no problems with the analyst, the professional problem-solver? So I said to him, 'You pretend to have no problems when in truth you have very big problems. You do this because you are not generous enough to allow that I might have the capacity to help not only Tony, but you also.'

My patient was badly shaken by this interpretation, but that evening he went and visited Tony and told him for the first time that he was having psychoanalysis for his problems. Tony felt greatly relieved that he was not the only problem in the family, and he persuaded Michael to tell his mother, which he did though reluctantly. Contrary to what he thought, his mother also felt greatly relieved, and she told him that she felt a mother to him for the first time for years, that she had always felt repudiated as a mother until then.

My patient had begun to construct a new world. He was not adjusting to the world, but was being a co-operative agent in the construction of a changing world, and in this he was open to others. This was a change in his soul from being passive to the destructive forces within, to co-opting these forces to work for his own constructive purposes. The analysis had been one of social adjustment, but was now a cure of soul.

There is some psychoanalysis that is concerned entirely with social adjustment; there is some the aim of which is the change of soul. However, there is much analysis which is a mixture of both. Some analysts have change of soul as a limited aim, but combine it with reassurance as a support to adjustment. Also, those who have change of soul as an aim fail to varying degrees to execute that aim. However, when I assert that psychoanalysis has the aim of rescuing the individual from the human condition I mean a change of soul analysis.

The particular sphere of the human condition that is encountered clinically is called narcissism, defined as a particular state of mind where the individual has taken his own ego as love object. Such a situation precludes compassion for others, which is the prime fruit of mature religious belief. Love, instead of being directed outwards towards others, is turned in upon the self. All motivation is governed by this principle. It is important to realize that this inner situation is not one that the subject realizes. In fact, frequently a person who is narcissistic will be devoted to people, for example, a great philanthropist, or devoted to good works; and yet he may be narcissistic. We need to understand this apparent contradiction, which is germane to the essence of psychoanalysis.

When someone has taken as love object his own ego he is not aware of it. In fact, he cannot be aware of it, and is forced to destroy knowledge of the situation. His perception, memory, imagination, judgement and beliefs are distorted by this inner configuration, and he is forced to compel reality to conform to this inner distortion.

For the narcissistic person there is no other in the inner emotional world. This is not known by the person himself, but comes to be realized by someone living on intimate terms with him. It is also a matter which comes to be revealed against much resistance in analysis. I will give some examples to illustrate the way in which someone can be unaware of the situation himself, although it is obvious, sometimes shockingly so, to another. Erich Fromm (1980) gives this example:

> A man called me to ask for an appointment. I answered that I had no free time in the week but could see him during the following week. He responded by pointing out that he lived very near to my office and hence it would take him little time to come over. When I answered that this was indeed convenient for him but it did not alter the fact that *I* had no free time, he was unimpressed and continued with the same argument.

And a few more examples:

> A man was very jealous when his wife flirted with a man at a party. When he had an affair with his secretary, his wife was dreadfully upset, but he was unable to understand why his wife should be upset.

> A woman believed that her analyst was in love with her, although the patient had seen her analyst with his wife and the analyst

had kept all the professional boundaries. The woman continued in her belief; all attempts to undeceive her failed.

A group of people on the way back from an outing had a coach crash. One girl's arm was smashed, and she was in considerable pain. A passing car immediately offered to take the girl to hospital. A man in the group insisted that the car make a deviation to drop him off at the house of a friend where he was expected for a party. When his request was greeted with shocked amazement, he raged and threw a tantrum.

The narcissistic person is unable to see something from the other person's point of view because the other does not exist emotionally. Taking the first example, Fromm's needs are felt by the man to be his own as those are the only ones that exist. In Kleinian terminology, Fromm is just a breast to feed the man-baby. Fromm has been accreted to the man's own ego, so in emotional perception there are not two persons but one, and this one is very inflated.

The cuckoo lays its eggs in the nest of another bird. As it outgrows the other birds in the brood, it flips them out of the nest. Such is the ego of the narcissistic person; it gets rid of all traces of the other. This begins to give us some idea of what is meant by 'emotional', which describes the activities of the ego in relation to the other in the internal world, and the resulting structure.

A clergyman once came to see me who was devoted to famine relief in the Third World. In the outer forum he was devoted to others; however, his wife left him because he had no interest in her. Her concerns were a frustration to him, she got in the way and was a nuisance to him. It emerged that inwardly she did not exist; instead she was incorporated into his inflated ego. So one of the elements of the emotional is the ego's inner relations to objects, but this is not a static state of affairs. This inner relation is only maintained through action; therefore there is an inner activity which we might describe in this way. The other is incorporated and this is an activity of the ego.

Self-knowledge comes about through comparison with the other. If I live in a small village on an island and there is no television or cinema, I have no awareness of the whiteness of my skin. I only become aware of it when I one day encounter a black man; I then realize something about myself which I had not realized before. If I am a Pygmy and live in the depths of the Ituri Forest in the Congo and have only seen members of my own tribe and one day I see a six-foot man from outside I realize that I am of smaller height. I can only learn about myself through being in relation to another. If I have incorporated the other inwardly and made them a part of myself, there is no one present, and I do not know myself because I need the other to be inwardly present in order to know myself. Using the Socratic principle, I cannot do evil and know I am doing it because if I know evil I will not do it. In *The Third Man*, Harry Lime was able to hide from the knowledge that his criminal activity was responsible for people's deaths by turning them into dots in his mind, for example when he takes Holly Martins up on the fairground wheel and points to the human beings below, visually they have been reduced to dots. This was a clever device of Graham Greene's because for a moment the viewer can understand Lime's rationalization. Then Major Calloway takes Holly Martins to a hospital where he sees young children dying in fearful pain as a result of using Harry Lime's diluted penicillin. When Holly Martins sees it from this perspective he can no longer go along with his friend's activities. Harry Lime had seduced him onto the top of the wheel where the human being as other was obliterated. When I destroy the other in my mind I make the other a dot, and so do not know about destruction because a dot is not an other.

This destruction of my mind is the fundamental disaster; it is the kernel of the human condition. This savaging of my mental processes and its relation to an ethical choice to destroy the other, the good, is what I want now to describe. It is my own personal theory of narcissism, which I have outlined in more detail in a recent book.

The hypothesis of primary narcissism is based on the belief that the infant is not object-related at the start of life. Instead, I follow the position taken by Klein, Winnicott and Fairbairn, and the whole British object relations school, which posits infantile relatedness from the beginning of life. This position has also been confirmed by researchers like Daniel Stern.

The only narcissism that exists is what is known as secondary narcissism, and it is this which will be referred to in the following. The classical theory of narcissism states that libido has taken its own self as love object. I am in agreement with the second part of that statement, that the ego or self has been taken as love object, but the question arises by whom?, or, by what? The word 'libido' is used to describe a drive towards attachment. When we see an infant 'naturally' pushing towards the mother's nipple, we unquestioningly say that this activity is instinctual, meaning there is no ego involved. It is this assumption that I wish to challenge. If the infant is object-related from birth, then the source of the activity towards the object is the ego; activity from the ego is by definition not instinctual. In order to gain some clarity about this, we need to reflect a bit more upon what we mean by object.

There was this difference between Melanie Klein and Anna Freud: Klein said that the infant was object-related from birth, and that there was an ego from this stage onwards, if only inchoate; Anna Freud said that at birth there was no ego, and that the infant's activity was instinctual and therefore found its source not in the ego but in what her father had named the id, and that the infant was in an objectless state at the beginning. Yet it is clear that an objectless state did not mean that the new infant did not attach itself to an object, and therefore an objectless state means a state in which there is no *mental* object. Anna Freud said there was only a sensual object at the start, and only later did this differentiate into a sensual object and then a mental object; Klein said that a mental object was present from birth onwards.

The source of action towards this mental object is the ego, and hence the object relations theorists also held that there was an ego from birth, and therefore a mental structure in place. However, at this point I depart from Melanie Klein in an important way. I say that in relation to the mental object there exists only intentional action, whose source is the ego. Klein, in order to explain anxiety, introduces the presence of instinct existing in the personality *as an object*. It is my view that instinctual action has been transformed in human beings into ego action, and therefore it is a regressive and illogical step to introduce instinct in the way that Klein does.

My position is closer to that of Fairbairn in that he did not envisage any source of emotional action within the personality other than the ego. For Fairbairn, anxiety was the product of a traumatizing outer agent, which I believe is also a mistaken view. However, even he did not follow the position which he had established through to its logical conclusion, the clue to this being his continued use of the word 'libido'. Libido is a thing, not a connective between ego and object. Libido is something apart from 'I wish', 'I want', or 'I desire'.

In the formulation that I am constructing here, we must dispense with the concept libido, and therefore the classical definition of narcissism as libido taking its own self or ego as object will not do. Instead, we must say that the ego takes its own self as love object. This means that a mental structure has been erected, and that the activity by which the ego has become its own love object is an intentional act. Fairbairn becomes illogical when, although he posits action as issuing from the ego, he does not make it intentional. If that is the case, then what is the criterion by which action from the ego is differentiated from action from the id? It seems clear that the difference is that action from the ego implies choice, whereas action from the id does not.

It is necessary to differentiate between conscious and unconscious choice, and I am referring here to the latter. There is a field of action in relation to the other, the mental object. There are possibilities within this field that are determined by the consequence to the other. An action always negates other possibilities. This is what is defined here as choice but it is not in consciousness that a change in action is felt. Such changes occur frequently within the analytic process and accounts of them can be read in clinical accounts in psychoanalytic literature.

This is a rather long diversion to explicate the classical definition of narcissism. We are now in a position to make the first point, which is simply that when the ego takes its own self as love object, this is a choice. The implication is that there were other possibilities, or at least one such possibility which was negated. It is this refused possibility that needs to be examined. The ego's object is mental; the choice of the mental object forms the structure which is the psychological being of the human. When the self is chosen as love object, the calamity is the negated possibility – what has *not* been chosen. The refusal of the mental object, that which has not been done – this is at the centre of the narcissistic condition. This constitutes the disaster which lies at the base of the psychic structure. The question is, 'What is the nature of this mental object?' As I am suggesting that this object as part of a structure constitutes the basis of mental health, we need to define what we mean by mental health.

In the course of a life, even the most sheltered individual meets crises along life's way. There are painful illnesses and accidents that occur in childhood, the deaths of parents or other family members, the pains of being rejected in love. There are the appalling national and international catastrophes of which some of us will be a part. Then there is the crisis of our own death in whatever form it may come. Life *is* a series of unavoidable crises that always involve pain and suffering. The person who is mentally healthy is the one who is able to face these crises, even to embrace them with fortitude, and win through to joy. Such a person relies on something within through which he or she will co-operate with others in the battle of life. I propose to call this inner quality the Lifegiver.

The Lifegiver is the name I am giving to the mental object which is negated in the state of narcissism, or chosen in the state of mental vigour. It is a mental object which only comes into existence in the act of being chosen. This sounds paradoxical, but there are parallels in our social world; for example, friendship only comes into being in the act of being forged – so also the Lifegiver is a mental object which comes into existence in the act of being chosen. The act through which the Lifegiver is chosen brings about this mental reality as an inner possession. The person has then the inner equipment necessary for the crises of life. What happens when the Lifegiver is refused?

The essence of narcissism lies in an emotional refusal. Being emotional, this refusal is at the bedrock of the personality, and therefore permeates all the decisions and action patterns of a lifetime. If there is a deep emotional refusal in the face of a crisis, the person never *meets* the crisis, and so is crushed by it rather than being able to surmount it. I believe that the classical definition of narcissism has failed to conceptualize this because it has concentrated upon the other element in this choice, the selection of the self as love object, which is secondary.

There is another consequence which is extremely important, and I believe not recognized in some schools of psychoanalysis. The consequence of this refusal is guilt, which is not available to consciousness. The situation occurs something like this. The initial refusal is repeated in all the contours of life's happenings. Each time, it is attended by guilt. This manifests itself in a variety of ways: people bring down on their head disasters of one sort or another, for example, they marry someone who everyone predicted would lead to disaster; they have a series of car accidents; they invest their money recklessly and so on.

Inwardly, people judge themselves to be bad – so bad that they cannot bear to experience it, so they have to seduce the world into telling them they are good. They find comforters in the outer world, whom they cannot do without, which means they are extremely dependent upon stroking from their companions. The typical example of this is the nice guy, who inwardly feels so bad that he cannot allow himself to experience it. The bad guy is got rid of, projected into a hated figure in his social world – his family, the boss at work, an organization. The force with which this bad inner guy is projected is frequently enormous; should it turn inwards, the individual experiences such a massive depression that he may kill himself.

Through failing to acknowledge this basic refusal of the Lifegiver, which lies at the heart of narcissism, many clinicians do not recognize that guilt and badness are an inherent part of the narcissistic clinical picture because outwardly the person presents himself as nice and devoted. It is not realized that when he needs frequent stroking from his family and friends it is because inwardly he feels intolerably bad. He therefore has to erect a barrier against those feelings, and substitute for his real feelings the false surface feelings generated by social stroking. He is cut off from himself, and what we encounter is a false façade that is the opposite to what the person inwardly feels; he cannot know what he feels because it brings him to awareness of the basic refusal of the Lifegiver, which is intolerable. And the more intolerable it is, the more does he assert with certainty the shockingness of the outer figure, which is a projection of his own perceived badness.

It is because the fundamental refusal of the Lifegiver has not been conceptualized in psychoanalytic thinking that many clinicians do not realize that this negativity is an inherent part of narcissism; it is part of its structure. It is a mistake to place negative and positive narcissism into two separate categories. If by positive narcissism someone means self-confidence or self-esteem, it leads to semantic confusion; narcissism undermines self-confidence. Negative narcissism which comes from this refusal is part and parcel of narcissism; positive narcissism is the false façade which we referred to just recently. We shall in a moment come to the compensatory choice that occurs when the Lifegiver is rejected.

It is clear that someone who is narcissistic is in a sorry condition psychologically. He is devoid, or nearly so, of access to the mental object which is the source of autonomous action. He is unable to create free response from within his human environment. He may bully people or pressure them to conform to his will, but this is the opposite of free creative action. The motive here is to force endorsement of his point of view. A person who has calm certainty within does not need to force a ratification of his view; the fact that it is *his* view is not of interest. The person who is not dominated by narcissistic currents is in relation to the point of view: he is not concerned to take possession of it. The Lifegiver is an object to which he has a relation if he has made the fundamental 'Yes'. It is a paradox that this 'Yes' gives him possession of the Lifegiver within, and yet he is not possessive of it.

It is necessary to refine what has been said about the refusal of the Lifegiver, for it is not possible for any human to refuse it utterly. For there to be life at all there has to be some acceptance, but this acceptance is overridden by the refusal. This is because the Lifegiver is an inner and outer object, and therefore the refusal is partly a refusal of the individual's own inner life. The refusal does not, however, entirely cancel out the inner life but fashions a tendency which is always there, the aim of which is the obliteration of the Lifegiver.

This leaves the psyche with a problem. The person does not have within the inner equipment necessary to negotiate the predicaments of life, and therefore takes another pathway to generating the energy he requires. Instead of opting for the Lifegiver, he takes his own self as love object.

Now, the self which is taken as love object is not a mental object but a sensuous object; the act of taking the self is a sensuous compensation for what has been lost. Through this action, the self is eroticized as essentially a pleasurable stimulation of surfaces. (Post-modernism, which is concerned with surfaces, I believe shows that the present-day culture in the Western world favours and endorses this aspect of narcissism.)

This stimulation of the self generates motivation, but it does not last. It is characterized by excitement which dies down, whereupon another burst of excitement is necessary. This kind of excitement can be of many kinds. It can be generated by getting drunk, by sexual orgy, by triumphing over a rival, by rousing the enthusiasm and adoration of a crowd. Sometimes it is done through generating the devotion and admiration of just one or two loyal disciples. An historical example of this would be the way in which Savonarola had the unfailing devotion of Fra Domenico right until the moment of their joint deaths.

However, the most powerful agent of eroticization is destruction: destruction is exciting. I once interviewed an adolescent boy who told me how he blew up the stump of a tree in his garden with a stick of dynamite. The gleam of excitement in his eye was unmistakable. Public executions always drew the crowds, just as violent films do today. American servicemen waiting to drop their atomic bomb on Nagasaki were in a fever of anxiety lest Japan surrender before they could drop their accursed weapon. This excitement at violent death, at destroying the beautiful, at smashing up the creativity and hopes of others applies equally to the person's own self. Just as the creative act is being born in the depths, so it is viciously attacked from within, and this generates excitement. It supplies a little fillip that gives another short period of motivation. Destructiveness to self and to others is an essential component of narcissism. It is therefore a condition of soul which is extremely injurious to humankind as individuals and to society. It is the very heart of the human condition.

It may appear from what has been said so far that efficient causes have no role in the formation of the narcissistic condition. Yet most psychoanalysts pay attention to the patient's life history and to the traumata that the individual has undergone in infancy. The child, the infant – nay, even the foetus – experiences pain. The young one has a relationship to the traumatic event, and there is a free element in this relationship. Narcissism is the decision to close off from the pain. In an analysis that aims at a cure of soul, a repetition of the original trauma arises again and again, and the individual has the opportunity to go down a different path. To choose the high ground involves excruciating pain. We can only applaud when

125

someone does so, and be sad when he or she does not. I was told once that during the Second World War when an English spy gave up secrets under torture not a word of reproach was uttered; when someone kept silent and did not reveal secrets even under torture he or she achieved heroism. Extreme pain pulls the individual towards narcissism. Narcissism is not, however, inevitable, because there are heroes.

The prime aim of psychoanalysis is to change the inner state of the individual, to transform narcissism. As a central problem, narcissism has come more and more to the fore in psychoanalytic literature in the last three decades. It is beginning to be recognized increasingly that if it is not tackled and transformed, then all we get is symptomatic relief. The reverse of this is also true: that nearly all psychopathology has its origin in narcissism. I believe that it can be demonstrated that schizophrenia, manic-depressive psychoses, hysterical disorders, obsessionality, psycho-pathy, depression and phobic conditions can all be traced back to narcissism. The demonstration of this proposition would require a book and also a lifetime's research, so the only pointer I will make here is that an essential aspect of narcissism is omnipotence. Sometimes it is very evident, but it is frequently hidden. Omnipotence is always present and is the effective agent in all the pathological conditions mentioned above. Omnipotence through which these disorders come about in the persona-lity is part of the structure of narcissism. It is through omnipotent action that denial, projection, splitting, coalescing, introjection, magnification, diminishment and fusion come about, and it is through differing combinations of these that all psychopathology originates.

I have tried to pinpoint certain core values which lie at the heart of all mature religion. In a similar way, I believe that the psychological core of the human condition is narcissism. There are today many who deplore, for example, the stockpiling of arms; the destruction of the rainforests; the seas that are plundered in order to provide gourmet meals. We shout and clamour from our pulpits with all the venom of the hell-fire preacher. I believe, however, that we shall make no progress in the transformation of the human condition until we understand that its root lies in the emotional state where the other does not exist; where reality is cancelled out; where a pseudo-self dominates the scenario. The hell-fire preacher has never cured the world of its ills; instead we need scientifically to examine their root cause, and when we understand it, then we may gain some power over it. Freud believed that if he could understand the structure of a neurosis then he had power over it. The same, I believe, applies to the human condition.

REFERENCES

Erich Fromm (1980) *Greatness and Limitations of Freud's Thought* (London: Jonathan Cape), p. 48.

Vladimir Soloviev (1918) *The Justification of the Good* (London: Constable and Company Ltd).

Daniel Stern (1985) *The Interpersonal World of the Infant* (New York: Basis Books).

Neville Symington (1993) *Lectures on Narcissism* (London: Karnac Books).

16

The Transformation of Narcissism through Psychoanalysis

What was there after all? Joy, fear, sorrow, devotion, valour, rage – who can tell? – but truth – truth stripped of its cloak of time. Let the fool gape and shudder – the man knows, and can look on without a wink. But he must at least be as much of a man as these on the shore. He must meet that truth with his own true stuff – with his own inborn strength.

(Conrad, 1973)

The core of psychoanalytic method is the use of the transference, a phenomenon whereby the patient expects the analyst to behave in preset ways. These are determined by the patient's inner mental states, which affect how the analyst is perceived. It is frequently stated in the analytic literature that these inner mental states are 'caused' by the ways in which people, especially parents, have behaved towards the patient in the infantile environment. What the analyst then experiences in the transference is a projection onto him of this parental imago but what becomes clear in the infantile situation is that the patient is identified with this imago. In other words what is transferred on to the analyst is a hated part of the patient's own self. This identification becomes known when the analyst can see that the patient is behaving in precisely the way that the parent is claimed to have behaved towards the patient.

Let us say, for example, that the patient says that his mother always interrupted him whenever he was engaged in a serious conversation, which infuriated him. The analyst notices that just when an important emotional matter is discovered in the session, the patient goes off on to some trivial red herring. It becomes clear that the mother who is hated for behaving like this is a part of the self acting in just the same frustrating way. It is a mode of acting that the patient hates because it prevents a moment of emotional insight and integration occurring. All this, however, only becomes clear in the patient's interaction and relationship with the

128

analyst, which is the catalyst that illuminates the parts of the self that block self-knowledge.

What we are saying, therefore, is that parts of the self can act against truth, against self-knowledge developing in the analytic relationship. It is also a fact that these parts of the self that act against self-integration are active in intimate relationships. So, for instance, in the example just given above, it is not only that the part of the self, the frustrating mother, interferes with integration, but that it also frustrates the analyst in his endeavour to understand. The activity that interferes with the patient's intrapsychic integration also disorganizes the analyst's process of reasoning. This is also what is meant by the transference: that the interference the analyst experiences is the outer manifestation of what is happening within the patient; what the analyst experiences is also occurring within the mind of the patient.

The conclusion we may draw from this is that the mental disruptions are not known directly by the individual, but only become known in relationship to the analyst because it is here that the inner processes are dramatized. Moreover, the inner mental processes can only be known in the context of an analytic relationship. Therefore it is precisely within the most intimate emotional relationship that the individual is challenged to confront the dark forces of his mind.

We need to give a name to the inner processes which interfere with self-knowledge and psychic integration. In the example given above, we have an internal mother who interferes with a fruitful coming together. We might give the name 'jealous' to such a mother, and therefore we would say that there is a jealous personality that is active within and that is interfering with and preventing insight and emotional understanding. There are other personalities within which are hostile to the development of self-knowledge and understanding. Another we could name 'greed'. An example of this in the clinical situation is when the analyst gives an interpretation which is helpful, but its helpfulness is impaired because the patient's inner eyes are focused upon the analyst's ability to interpret, which he greedily wants. This desire to have this ability for himself overrides his desire to understand. Greed is a metaphor borrowed from a quality which can be observed in eating. All the language of the emotions which we use is metaphors, and this is another.

Within the personality, then, there are patterns of functioning which interfere with mental illumination or insight. Ultimately, these interfere with the acquisition of wisdom, preventing us from reaching a knowledge of how to live. The desire to acquire this wisdom is a spiritual goal; psychoanalysis serves this spiritual goal, but its methodology is different from traditional spiritualities. The methodology of the latter has been through introspection: the person seeking holiness has drawn apart from the crowd, and sought it through personal introspection. He may and probably would get guidance from a spiritual director, but he would not seek knowledge of the interior life *in* the relationship.

Mental jamming of the type described occurs *in* the relationship. When in analysis something becomes unjammed it has an effect intrapsychically and interpersonally. The two are interlinked: the unsticking of one unsticks the other also. Each time an inner obstacle is removed there comes about an emotional deepening.

These inner obstacles are like vicious personalities attacking the process of integration. They are part of the structure of narcissism. They are the agglomerated person who has refused the Lifegiver, constituting that part of the personality that is against itself. We saw in the previous chapter that the Lifegiver *is* the emotional life of the individual. The refusing part of the personality is what is met in the analysis as resistance, which is made up of an association of personalities.

A psychoanalyst is always up against resistance to the process, and, as the analysis proceeds, the resistance frequently becomes stronger. It is a well-known phenomenon that a particularly powerful resistance arises just as there is a move towards new integration. This is known clinically as the negative therapeutic reaction. As an analysis proceeds, the resistance becomes subtler. The analysis is an ongoing battle against resistant aspects of the personality, bearing all the notes of the spiritual struggle described by mystics both in Western and Eastern religious cultures. The struggle is an all-out attempt to reverse the early infantile option I have called narcissistic.

The spiritual struggle takes place in psychoanalysis *within* the relationship. It is also within the relationship that the dark forces – Mara in Buddhist thinking; Satan in Christian theology; the Shadow in Jungian psychology – become revealed. It is in the personal encounter that the patient and the analyst meet the disowned parts of the patient. The patient projects the disowned parts of himself, those dark forces, into the analyst. By not turning away, he meets them in his encounter with the analyst. The greatest spiritual struggles with himself occur in the moments of greatest confrontation between himself and the analyst. (This aspect of the analytic relationship has been particularly emphasized by the American analyst Harold Searles.)

That the greatest spiritual encounters occur in the emotional confrontation with the analyst is a momentous fact that has not been registered either by theologians or by psychoanalysts. It has not been because they do not recognize that psychoanalysis is a spiritual endeavour. Theologians, with some reason, believe that psychoanalysis is an anti-religious movement in modern culture, and psychoanalysts themselves are anxious that their discipline not be tainted with any religiosity.

The fact that I meet the dark side of myself in the personal encounter with my analyst has an enormous significance when the following is considered. My analyst is trained to reveal the dark side of myself to myself, but the meeting of this side of myself occurs in relation to my analyst. The only way in which the encounter with the analyst differs from encounters with significant others in my life is that the analyst helps me in the work of revealing my disowned emotional activity. However, as I begin to internalize the analytical function inside myself, I come to meet my disowned self in all the other significant encounters of my life. They are significant in terms of their emotional closeness. It is in my mother and father, in brothers and sisters, in spouse or partner, in daughters and sons that I meet my disowned self. I am forced in each encounter either into relation with myself, or I repeat the archaic refusal and turn away. Thus the deepest spiritual struggle occurs in relation to my intimates. It is a spiritual struggle that is quite the opposite to that where the person who strove for spiritual perfection went out into the desert, away from all intimate relationships.

In the introduction I said it is my belief that the reason for the present malaise in the world of today is the collapse of those core values which have been central to mature religions for the last two-and-a-half millennia; also that these values do not connect with the modes of existence proper to modern man. The contempt, hatred and cruelty that are enacted emotionally between man and woman, parents and children are *the* relevant spiritual locus in present-day structures of living. Psychoanalysis recognizes that *this* is the locus for transforming action. Traditional religion, despite all its attempts, has failed to cross the bridge from the *fuga mundi* spirituality to one that is truly incarnate in the world.

What characterizes modern man is a need to be able to negotiate close emotional relationships. A great deal has been written on this topic, from many different angles. Here I will approach it from the perspective in which I encounter it.

In the early decades of this century, patients came for psychoanalysis suffering from recognized psychiatric conditions: hysteria, obsessionality, phobias or depression. Today most patients come because of a failure in relationships. In traditional society, based on the extended family, there was group accommodation of the individual, so that the orientation of the personality was accommodated within the group. There was a certain distance between one individual and another, and each was able to live within that allotted circumference. It was not required of the individual that he satisfy the emotional demands of his intimates; he was only required to do his work within certain bounds. A wife was bound to gather in vegetables from the plot of land, to rear her husband's children, to feed the family, to cook, to satisfy her husband's sexual demands, and so on. However, her husband could not require that she relinquish her infantile attachment to her parents and develop a mature love for him. In traditional society the husband was expected to till the land, tend the horses, sow and harvest the crops, maintain the buildings and provide for his family. All this his wife could expect of him, but she could not expect him to renounce his Oedipal attachment to his parents. This level of emotional commitment was not expected – but in modern man this is required.

The habitat of modern man is the city. Here, he lives typically in an apartment block, divorced from nature, divested of his ancient heritage. His feet do not tread the soil but rather the concrete that covers the earth like a baked clay from which all signs of fertility have been banished. In this world where he and she are dispossessed of natural satisfactions, he demands emotional compensation. When he had the beauty of a sunset amid the autumn leaves to imbue his soul with wonder, it did not worry him that his wife ignored him in favour of their newborn child. Indeed, he did not even notice but it acted as an unconscious spur to mend the roof and attend to other bits of maintenance which heretofore he had neglected. But place this same man in the modern apartment block, with no sunset, no cows to milk, and a wife who has turned emotionally from him, and he ricochets hopelessly into drink, gloomy slumping in front of the television, or a sexual affair with his secretary. With his unresolved Oedipal attachments, he is lonely, like a rudderless ship in an aimless sea. It is required of modern man that he cut the umbilical cord, that he overcome his childlike clingings.

When his wife has given birth to their newborn child, what is required of this husband is that he give emotionally to her. He needs within him that mental object we have insisted upon, his own inborn strength. His own need to be loved is the heart of narcissism, and if he is narcissistic he does not have the inner strength to carry him through the crisis of the new birth, wherein his wife's affections are turned towards their son. Maturity requires that he allow those affections to be directed towards his son. It is demanded of him that he detach himself from the need for that sensual affection of which the baby is now the recipient. He needs to be detached from this so that he can give emotionally, not to God, but to his wife. It is a spiritual programme of detachment in order to be able to give. It is giving at this level of emotional action.

The detachment required of him is detachment from a reality that exercises a sensuous attraction: the pleasant feeling of being loved and stroked; of being the special one. In this case it is required of the husband to become detached from this sensuous need, from this need to be caressed. He is required to become detached from it, but at the same time remain as husband and become the emotional giver. This is an exacting spirituality, requiring a detachment no smaller than that advocated by St John of the Cross; it is nothing less than a Dark Night of the Senses. The comfortable feeling of being caressed has to be renounced; that feeling of being the only one – it is required of the husband that he bear this and not go off in a sulk.

The detachment from these comfortable feelings is in order to be able to give emotionally. This means that his situation requires co-operative giving, an unseen giving. Although it manifests itself in physical supports of all kinds, emotional giving is not to be equated with these. It is a primitive, mental giving that arises from the other as a person being present. If the individual is narcissistic and therefore does not have this mental source within, then his assumption is that the other is there to stimulate him, excite him, praise him, and ultimately to motivate him. He looks to the other to be the source of action for him, through arousing him in sensuous ways.

This self-stripping of sensuous desires in order to be free for emotional giving is *the* self-discipline required of us. It is because we are divested of other means of giving that this remains the only one. Partners both earn money, cook, clean the house, service the car, attend to the bills and financial accounts. There may be some division of labour in these activities, but it is becoming more and more common and assumed among modern couples that they are each able to perform any of these tasks. The only area left for the man and the woman is that of emotional giving, and it is this that they require of their partner.

I feel it necessary to emphasize the level at which the phrase 'emotional giving' is used. It is most emphatically not at the level of words: a person may talk of 'concern', 'caring' or 'compassion' but be utterly devoid of emotional giving. The hypocrite is the person who proclaims these virtuous attitudes but acts differently. The level of acting that I am trying to describe is particularly difficult because it is a mental level that is based on an inner structure. There is only one measure of it: feelings over an extended time period. I will now take both elements in this statement and subject them to examination.

I meet John Smith and I feel cautious. The feeling of caution arises through my encounter with John Smith. After he has left my house, I may observe that John Smith was very polite, took a great interest in the project I was discussing with him, asked after my mother who was ill at the time, and offered to deliver a parcel to a friend. He did not do anything of which I could complain – and yet I felt cautious. This feeling has been generated by John Smith at the level of action which I call emotional. John Smith was doing something. When I try to understand my own caution, I can only pin down one seemingly insignificant incident: the reason for my meeting with John Smith is that he is going to rent my house for six months while I go abroad. Everything in our discussion seemed eminently reasonable, and it seemed that in all matters of finance he would be fair-minded. However, at one point he said in a joking aside that when he has to telephone a friend overseas, he always picks a time when the friend will be out and leaves a message on his answering machine requesting him to ring back. Then John Smith said with evident delight, 'So, you see, it's the overseas friend that has to pay for the call.' This, I realize, was the remark that made me cautious. When I say this, my wife adds that she had not liked the way he glanced furtively at our display cabinet with weasel-like eyes. So these were the two signals that gave rise to this feeling of caution. However, it is important to note that these signals were the *carriers* of an emotional message. It is not the signals themselves, but the emotional current, the emotional activity of which these signals are only the carriers.

The feelings which are registers of this area of the emotional can be most subtle. In *The Heart of Darkness*, Conrad says this about a character:

He was of middle size and ordinary build. His eyes, of the usual blue, were perhaps remarkably cold, and he certainly could make his glance fall on one as trenchant and heavy as an axe. But even at these times the rest of his person seemed to disclaim intention. Otherwise there was only an indefinable, faint expression of his lips, something stealthy – a smile – not a smile – I remember it, but I can't explain. It was unconscious, this smile was, though just after he had said something it got intensified for an instant. It came at the end of his speeches like a seal applied on the words to make the meaning of the commonest phrase appear absolutely inscrutable. He was a common trader, from his youth up employed in these parts – nothing more. He was obeyed, yet he inspired neither love nor fear, nor even respect. He inspired uneasiness. That was it! Uneasiness.

In clinical discussions among psychoanalysts and psychotherapists someone will often say, 'I picked up his envy', or 'I picked up his fear', or 'I picked up his ruthlessness', and so on. Here is a more conscious focusing for the purposes of treatment of the universal judgement that human beings make through their feelings. Feelings, then, are the human inventory of the unseen emotional actions, which are at a very elemental level. It is the activity at this level that is crucial in the sphere of human intimacy.

This brings us to the second element in our definition: feelings *over an extended period of time*. It takes time to get in touch with our deeper feelings. In the cases quoted above, the feelings of caution and uneasiness were registered rapidly, but deeper feelings that register this level of emotional action take time to register. The time period may be weeks, months or years. It is often some years into a marriage that one spouse comes to know the other. There is probably an evolutionary reason for this: the orientation of our perception is geared to the outer world for survival's sake. The turning of perception inwards to this inner register of the emotional activity is against the ancestral pull of survival. So an extended period of time is required for this feeling barometer to register at the deeper levels of emotional action. The psychoanalyst Elliott Jaques has shown convincingly that the measure of the work required in such cases is in the time taken for the task to be fulfilled.

The place where spiritual light is needed in the modern world is where emotional action operates. The spiritualities within traditional religion do not encompass this level of emotional action. I have on occasions given papers on this topic, and it has been claimed that the spirituality of Judaism does encompass this sphere. I believe this to be an error based on a misunderstanding. The focus of Judaism is on the virtues of family life: love, affection and loyalty in the deepening knowledge of God. The severe command to leave family and friends and meet God in the desert is totally foreign to Judaism. Detachment as a spiritual goal plays less part in Judaism than it does in Christian and Buddhist spirituality. However, the darker forces in us that operate in emotional action towards those with whom we are intimate occur just as much within Judaism as they do in families of all cultures. The idea that we meet these dark forces in our encounter with our intimates is as foreign to Judaism as to other traditional religions. What we discover in psychoanalytic investigation is that when we are engaged in a collusion with the dark forms within us, we are held to it by a well-nigh irresistible attraction. It is because it is crucial that we become liberated from this 'fatal attraction' that the kernel of true spirituality lies in detachment.

In Christianity and Buddhism detachment has been equated with a severing of family ties, with the consequent view that the highest pinnacles of spiritual development are to be found in the monastery or the convent. This remains so despite the enormous emphasis in recent years upon spirituality among lay people. In Judaism, on the other hand, closeness to God is to be found in the family, and therefore its spiritual accent appears to be the exact opposite of Christianity and Buddhism. However, although detachment is not emphasized within Judaism, yet detachment from emotional cruelty, hatred and contempt, which are linked to the need for sensual attachment, is a central religious goal. Therefore in Christianity, Buddhism and Judaism the detachment from the sensual object is lacking in the emotional sphere. This applies also to Hinduism in this respect.

Detachment thus has either been applied to the wrong goal, or not sufficiently developed within traditional religion. It has, of course, been central within mystical devotion, but it has always been believed that the heights of mysticism are only possible in one who has severed all emotional ties. It is the thesis of this book that the field for mystical union with the Ultimate is within the closest emotional bonds.

Without spiritual detachment, religion is always in danger of becoming identified with concrete objects. There are many radical churchpeople today whose 'welfare religion' utterly fails to reach the core of today's malaise. St Ignatius of Loyola, who founded the Jesuits and devoted his whole life to their establishment, said that if the Jesuits were suppressed by the Pope, he would after a quarter of an hour of prayer think no more about it. Aldous Huxley quotes this in his book *The Perennial Philosophy*, and goes on to say that the most difficult of all mortifications is the achievement of a holy indifference to temporal success or failure of a cause to which one has devoted one's best energies. However, it is precisely this detachment which raises an activity from the sphere of social welfare to that of a spiritual religion.

We meet the dark side of ourselves *in* the close encounter with our intimates. It is in this daily encounter that we are faced with the greatest spiritual struggles. It is no longer in the desert that we meet our inner adversary, but in our daily emotional encounters. We do not become whole if we do not accept the dark side of ourselves. Jung said, 'The patient does not feel himself accepted unless the very worst in him is accepted too.' Melanie Klein said that if the bad in oneself is repudiated, then in that very act of repudiation the good, creative potential in oneself is also rejected and not available for use. I have witnessed this on many occasions in the clinical situation.

The transformation of narcissism through psychoanalysis

We must therefore enter the struggle with the dark forces within us in order to initiate creative action within our social environment, in order to tap into what is most individual, most creative, and most fertile for the human community within our nature. We need to make contact with the Lifegiver that is always present in the depths. That basic refusal of the Lifegiver is never entirely repudiated; the struggle with the Shadow is against those dark forces which try to prevent us saying 'Yes' to the Lifegiver within us. It is this struggle with which psychoanalysis is concerned. As a spiritual method relevant to the modern world it needs to come out of the ghetto in which it is enclosed at the present time. Before this can happen, however, its spiritual nature must be recognized.

REFERENCES

Joseph Conrad (1973) *The Heart of Darkness* (Harmondsworth: Penguin Books), pp. 30–1, 52.
Aldous Huxley (1980) *The Perennial Philosophy* (London: Chatto & Windus), p. 120.
Elliott Jaques (1982) *The Form of Time* (United States: Crane, Russak & Co. Inc./ Britain: Heinemann Educational Books).
C. G. Jung (1984) *Modern Man in Search of a Soul* (Ark Paperbacks; London: Routledge), p. 270.
L. N. Tolstoy (1986) *Anna Karenin*, translated by Rosemary Edmonds (Harmondsworth: Penguin Books), pp. 242–3.

PART FOUR

In this section we look at the sphere in which the modern world most urgently needs to start the work of regeneration. Never in history has the human race possessed such marvels of technological accomplishment, and yet never has the predicament of man been more appalling. He has weapons which can many times wipe out all life on earth; he is rapidly depleting the natural resources of the planet and polluting those that remain. Famines on a vast scale occur in one country after another in the Third World which shame the inhabitants of the developed countries. There has been a massive increase in the crime rate in Western nations, drug-taking has also soared in all these countries and unemployment has reached alarming proportions, but what is most striking is the inability of governments to grasp the source of these problems.

All the horrors that beset us daily in the newspapers are symptoms of a sickness. This sickness, I believe, is our emotional impoverishment, the root of which lies in our relations of intimacy. If this foundation stone is not put to rights, then all else will fail. Traditional religion has failed not because it does not possess the values which are essential for the work of regeneration, but because it has failed to insert them into the emotional life of the modern world. In this last section, our attempt is to show that psychoanalysis inhabits the sphere where these core values of mature religion need to be, and where at the present time they are so painfully lacking. The goal of psychoanalysis, which is the healing of mental illness, cannot be achieved without bravely embracing these core values.

17

The Domain of Psychoanalysis

Religion is about an aspect of this world to which we are usually blind.

(Macmurray, 1936)

The domain of psychoanalysis is built upon three poles: an activity, an object and a subject. Knowledge of these three poles is essential to an understanding of psychoanalysis. Equally important are the manifestations of transference and counter-transference. We start with activity.

A patient comes for psychoanalysis because he suspects he is responsible in part for the problems which are hampering his life. Responsibility refers to those activities which find their origin in him but of which he is unaware. Psychoanalysis is the elucidation of those activities of which the patient (and probably the analyst) is unaware. What are these activities?

Freud made a distinction between those things which we are able to be aware of but are not, and those things which we actively oppose being aware of. I may not at this moment be aware of my breathing in and out because I am intent on typing, but there is no activity forbidding such an awareness. The breathing of which I am unaware is morally neutral. In a similar way, as I am typing a plane flies overhead, but I am unaware of it until my son comes into my room and draws my attention to it. Again, the plane flying overhead has no moral category attached to it. It is a fact of which I am unaware. The plane and the breathing are morally neutral. Activities of which I am unaware Freud named preconscious. Activities whose awareness I actively oppose Freud named the unconscious.

In what is known as the topographical model, Freud described the unconscious as though it were a stationary piece of territory. False imagery blocks the act of comprehension. This image of a solid something to be investigated has perverted our understanding and prevented us from reflecting correctly on what an analyst experiences in the consulting-room. In his later structural model, Freud did to some extent correct the static bias of the topographical model, but he never erased the latter from his theoretical system, and it continues to influence analysts from generation to generation.

What the analysis does is to make manifest *activities* of which the patient had until then been unaware. Also, the patient *actively* sets out to prevent the analyst from revealing these activities. This latter activity is not known. The question is, what are these activities whose knowledge the patient actively opposes?

I want first to give some examples of activities which became elucidated in the course of analyses.

A young man who was a clergyman entered analysis because he had not been able to marry. He was exceedingly suspicious of his analyst, whom he distrusted and feared. He had had several girlfriends, but when it got near to marriage the girl would break off relations with him. It later emerged that he was an isolated man with no close friends. Because of his church commitments, the analyst had given him lunch-time appointments on each day. It emerged later that the 'church commitments' which made psychoanalysis at any other time impossible were imaginary: they had been engineered by the patient in order to be able to feel he had the analyst's special time to himself.

The reasons given for the patient's request were a deceit to himself and to the analyst. He was not aware that the reasons were illusory. That there was a person in him who deceived himself and others was a very unwelcome piece of knowledge, and he *actively* disowned this deceitful part of himself. It further emerged that girlfriends broke off with him because they had felt deceived by him in ways not dissimilar to the way in which the analyst had been. When the analyst realized that it had not been necessary to give the clergyman lunch-time appointments he felt annoyed.

In one session, the patient asked himself why it was that he kept at such a distance emotionally from everyone. The analyst made this interpretation, 'When you disown this deceitful one in you it sets up a template for your relations with all the people outside of yourself also: your girlfriends, your parishioners, your analyst and your family.' The patient had therefore also been unaware of the *action* whereby he disowned an aspect of his own personality. His *activities* in relation to this part of himself were responsible for his social alienation. For shorthand, we shall call this the clergyman example.

The domain of psychoanalysis

A woman came for analysis because she had attacks of asthma and bronchitis, and her GP thought there was a psychosomatic element involved. She experienced the analyst as a possessive, demanding woman. After a year in analysis, one weekend she developed bad bronchitis. The following weekend she had an asthma attack. A pattern began to be assumed in these attacks: they occurred invariably at weekends, the days on which she had no sessions with the analyst. If she passed another patient on her way into the session she developed a cough during the session. When the analyst was with another person she hated it. The bronchitis, the asthma attacks and the cough were the language of the hatred. There was another phenomenon which the analyst noticed. When the analyst and her patient had just understood something extremely important, the analyst would feel together with her patient. However, the analyst would then notice that she felt adrift, cut off, and in a haze. The analyst concluded that as soon as the analyst and the patient had a moment of mutual understanding, there was a split-off part of the patient that violently attacked. In the language of this analysis, this jealous part of the patient was named Baby Gwendolen, and it was Baby Gwendolen who *actively* attacked the analyst's contentment in understanding. We shall refer to this as the Baby Gwendolen example.

Another woman patient was exceedingly deferential towards her analyst, believing he was very eminent and that she must therefore be extremely polite to him at all times. She told the analyst almost daily how wonderful he was and what marvellous things he was doing for her. However, the analyst felt something quite different: that he had not done anything for her, and consequently felt hopeless, that his capacity to give something emotionally to her had been paralysed. As he observed the process more acutely, he found that when he was thinking out a way of formulating an insight his mind became all fuzzy and he felt despairing. It emerged over time that she believed she was the centre of the universe. There was a deferential exterior, but another person inside this woman of whom she was not aware, who paralysed his mind. We shall call this the Deferential Lady.

What is one to call the activity in these three examples? We have established that the patients in all cases were unaware of the activity, but how is this activity to be categorized? It is not motor activity, though it may be embodied within motor activity; it is not intellectual activity. When we ask whether it is activity pertaining to the imagination we are closer to locating what structures it, what gives it form – but we have not defined the *it* or said what the *it* is. What is this invisible activity of which we are unaware? What is it that registers this activity? It is not seen, not heard and not touched, but it is *felt*. It is registered in the feelings, although the feeling may not be known.

In the Baby Gwendolen example, the analyst's feeling of contentment in the mutuality of understanding was attacked. It took time for the analyst in this case to be aware of her own feelings, to be aware of what was being done to her inner experience of mutuality. So the activity is registered in the feelings of the analyst, but what is the nature of the activity of which the feelings are a register? The activity is not known directly through the senses. It is clear that it is part of what makes the relationship between the analyst and the patient, and one of the elements that makes this relationship difficult for the analyst is the undermining quality of the activity.

Sometimes we talk of a business relationship, at other times we talk of a purely professional relationship. On each occasion we mean to imply that an element to be found in other relationships is not present. (We can leave to one side for the moment the fact that no relationship is ever devoid of the element we are in search of.) So what is the missing element of which these activities are a constituent part? The word we are in search of is 'emotional', meaning 'moving out from'. It is an activity that effects changes of mental states in the other person. This change of mental state is registered in the feelings, but the activity which we describe as emotional is not a feeling in itself. A thermometer registers heat, but is not heat itself – so also a feeling registers emotional activity, but is not the activity itself. Frequently the two are used interchangeably, but this leads to much confusion. The wide range of feelings register the variegated effects of emotional activity.

The examples I have given so far are restricted to activities which damage mental capacities. In the clergyman example the analyst felt annoyed because his belief had been undermined. In Baby Gwendolen the analyst's understanding state was shattered; and in the Deferential Lady, the analyst's hope was torpedoed. This is only the smallest sample of the effects of emotional activity; there are many others: in one emotional encounter my imagination is strangled; in another my memory is blotted out; in another my thinking is paralysed; in another my judgement is interfered with; in another my perception plays tricks on me, and so on. All the examples I have given are negative effects. This is because there is usually a predominance of damaging emotional activity in people who seek out psychoanalysis. There is also constructive emotional activity, but this is strangled to the extent to which the damaging emotional activity predominates.

When the analyst made the interpretation to the clergyman about his disowning relation to the deceitful one within setting the pattern for all outer relationships, the man was quiet and thoughtful and appeared to take in what had been said to him. That very evening two things occurred which were unusual. First, he and his girlfriend became more 'together' than they had ever been; second, a parishioner approached him about a sexual problem, which he had never dared to do before. The analyst noticed that in the subsequent session the patient was more open with him, and the analyst felt encouraged. We posit that the girlfriend felt more trustful of the clergyman as did the parishioner. Constructive emotional activity replaced destructive emotional action. All that I have said about negative effects can be said about positive effects: in one encounter my imagination is fired; in another my memory becomes clearer; in another my thinking becomes more concentrated; in another my judgement becomes more accurate; and in another my perception more pellucid.

I stress that these beneficial effects are not the result of encouraging remarks or praise but of *invisible emotional action*. When a patient's mental life improves during an analysis it is partly because of the analyst's positive constructive emotion. The analyst can also be the recipient of the patient's positive constructive emotion. I have given talks on this subject and realized that my audience have misunderstood the level at which I am talking. I am fearful that the same will be true of my reader.

The illustrations I have given are those which occur between psychoanalyst and patient because it is the locus *par excellence* where emotional action is examined. What is manifested in this situation are the activities that occur in all relationships throughout the human community. The relevance of this is particularly great among people between whom there are intimate bonds, for it is here that emotional action is more powerful and intense. We are looking, then, at *the* basic activity that occurs between one person and another. It is this activity of which people are frequently unaware, and from this unseen emotional activity relationships are forged. This is the unconscious activity or process which psychoanalysis investigates.

When the analyst made the interpretation to the clergyman about the deceitful part within him setting the pattern for all his outer relationships, something constructive occurred. The interpretation of the analyst did not hit a button which automatically produced the constructive changes; the interpretation was taken in, thought about unconsciously, and acted upon. Therefore, both negative and positive emotional activities are intentional in character. This is in accord with Freud's structural model in which a portion of the ego is unconscious. This means that the individual is unaware of a range of activities whose source is in the ego. It is only in view of this fact that it is possible for changes to occur within the psychoanalytic process, for if activities are not intentional they cannot be changed.

In the three examples above, the analyst experienced a feeling: with the clergyman he felt annoyed about the deception; with Baby Gwendolen she felt adrift and in a haze; and in the Deferential Lady he felt hopeless. These three sets of feelings are registrations of three different emotional action patterns of which the analyst is the *object*. Something is being *done to* the object: in the clergyman the analyst's trust is being undermined; in Baby Gwendolen the analyst's capacity to think is attacked; and in the Deferential Lady the analyst's hope is undermined. It would be possible to marshal examples where memory is eroded, judgement impaired, perception perverted, and so on. These are all actions being *done to* a person's mind, and if my mind is my most precious possession, then this is a very serious injury to sustain.

Traditional religion has become irrelevant because it has no knowledge of this activity. If I corrupt another's mind I am damaging him very seriously; if I corrode his hope I do him a great injury; if I erase his memory I do him serious harm. In all these cases I am not aware of what I am doing, yet the object is being damaged. I cannot opt out of this; I cannot turn aside from the human community so as to avoid this harm because in the very act of turning away I damage the other's confidence, or his hope, or his trust, as well as other mental faculties – and I am unaware of these activities. A person may devoutly attend to his religious duties as his faith defines them. He may be a very good neighbour, always ready to help in a crisis, may give of his time and money to various organizations – but his unconscious activity may be extremely destructive. Those who know about it will be his partner, his children, his parents, his brothers and sisters, his mistresses and those who rub up close to him at work. But the one person who will not know about it is the person himself. The reason for this is the operation of guilt. In order to understand this, we shall look at the object from the viewpoint of the seers of the Upanishads.

When I attack the mind of the object I reap guilt, because when I attack the reality in the other I also attack it in myself. I have seen this verified almost daily in the analyst's consulting-room. When the analyst's mind is being attacked, it is a sign that the patient's mind is being similarly attacked from within. The mind can be divided against itself and attack its own capacities. When the analyst feels despairing and realizes that his memory is being eroded, this experience gives him the knowledge that a split-off part of the patient's mind is attacking the patient's own mind and capacities. Another way of putting this is to say that interpersonal activity is a manifestation of intrapsychic action. Feelings, as we have seen, are the registration of emotional action from another. Conscience is the registration of negative emotional action towards my own self. Emotional action stirs feelings in another, but conscience is in myself. When I disregard conscience, the harvest I reap is guilt.

Thus guilt is the product of negative emotional action. It is a feeling that registers the damage sustained in myself by myself, the injury done to my own mind. This is what psychoanalytic investigation reveals, but it is not how the individual believes things to be who believes he has sustained an injury from an outside figure. The matter is complicated by the fact that the outer figure may have injured me, but this does not produce guilt. The guilt is produced by the damage I do to myself. Although I will often do this damage in relation to another, I will believe that it is done by the other. I am therefore aware neither of the negative emotional action towards my own mind, nor of the damage which I have done. To become aware of the damage I have done, I must also become aware of the negative emotional action that has wrought it. The consequence is that I am unaware of my guilt, and blame others for the ills that afflict me. I become self-righteous, or filled with self-pity, or I play the martyr.

The central locus of my unawareness is negative emotional action towards my own self. It is a psychological principle that negative emotional action towards my own mind always has damaging effect on positive emotional action. This is what I am unaware of, and what I resist becoming conscious of; this is the sphere that psychoanalysis investigates.

Mature religion is concerned with how we should live and act towards our neighbour and towards ourselves. This was the central message of Amos, Isaiah and Jesus in the Judaeo-Christian religion, and of the Buddha in the Far East. The reality in which I and the entire human community participate has an ultimate value, and this has a claim upon me. My manner of acting towards myself and others is therefore the central concern of mature religion.

Jews, Christians, Muslims, Hindus and Buddhists are all gathered together in a big hall to attend a special ecumenical service. The doors of the *aula* are shut, and suddenly they hear someone knocking loudly on the door. At first they ignore it, but eventually one of their number goes to the door and opens it. He finds a stranger standing there. He has a grey beard and hair, and wears glasses; he looks like a professor. He walks in and goes directly to the pulpit, from where he proclaims loudly, 'You who are gathered here desire to act correctly towards your neighbour, yet of the most important actions you know nothing.'

At first there are fierce cries, and some members of the congregation shout at him and demand that this importunate stranger be taken out. However, just as five able-bodied men – a Jew, a Christian, a Muslim, a Hindu, and a Buddhist – are about to pull him from the pulpit, one member of the congregation stands up and cries, 'Let him have a hearing! We have not heard yet what he has to say. If we are all blind, let him remove the scarves from our eyes.'

A silence falls upon the congregation, and the stranger begins to speak in a quiet, melodious voice that holds the attention of all present. This is what he says:

'I believe that all of you here sincerely wish to behave well towards your neighbour, that you wish to treat him with respect, that the human person has the very highest value in your scale of priorities. When you have given bread to the poor, spoken charitably of your neighbour, gone out of your way to help a friend who has suffered a bereavement, you come home and find that your wife is petulant and offhand. Something is wrong and you don't know what it is. You think perhaps she is premenstrual, or that one of your children has been rude to her. Later that night she lets fly at you. She says that you don't care about her, that you came home and didn't even ask her whether her job interview had gone well that day; you just ignore her; you expect her to have a meal ready and she gets no recognition for it, and she is fed up of it.

'You get all hot under the collar and say you have done no such thing, she has no right to accuse you so unfairly, and you go out of your way to treat her as a husband should. However, she asserts that this is how she feels. You say angrily that she has no right to feel that way. She answers quietly that whether she should feel it or shouldn't, it is what she feels.

'When you have calmed down later in the evening your wife speaks to you quietly. She tells you that you used to kiss her before you went to work but no longer; that before making love to her you would caress her and now you no longer do; that you used to thank her for meals she cooked but you no longer do; that you used to speak to her about work but you no longer do. She goes on to say to you that these are not the thing-in-itself but the signs of an attitude of yours. She feels treated as an object, just a piece of furniture, to be used. You have great difficulty understanding all

148

this, but after several further conversations you have some realizations which you reluctantly have to acknowledge seem to confirm what your wife is saying. You remember a colleague at work saying to you, "Doesn't your wife mind when you go to comfort your bereaved friend instead of going home to her?" You have to acknowledge to yourself that you have been treating her disrespectfully; you have not been aware of it, but you have not set a high value upon her, and she has felt it. In words you speak highly of your wife, but emotionally you obliterate her personhood.

'It is of this emotional way of acting that I want to speak to you all tonight. This is my invisible way of acting towards my wife, my children, my parents, my friends, and all those close to me. It is this manner of action which is the most important. Let me try to explain it in this way. Let us imagine a husband and wife again. They both have good jobs. The husband is an economist and works for the government, and the wife is a solicitor. They both earn about the same amount of money; they share the cooking and all the household chores. The husband is better at mathematics but the wife is a better administrator. The division of labour in the home is apportioned according to these varying personal capacities, and not according to traditional gender stereotypes. When these differing abilities are categorized they balance each other and are roughly equal in their personal level of social achievement and maturity. The husband is not needed to provide money because his wife earns money also; the wife does not have to do the cooking and ironing because her husband can and does do these. Can they give anything to each other? There is only one thing: they can give emotionally to each other. This giving is a something; it is real. It cannot be seen, measured, or heard, but it is real. Something is being given. If they fail in this then there is nothing. In traditional society the gender roles held the marriage structure together. In modern society, where these fixed gender roles are vanishing, then there is only one thing that this husband and wife and give to each other: positive emotional action. I call it positive constructive emotion. It is this that gives meaning to the marriage; meaning is the word we use to describe this reality.

'Very often a husband and wife can live together and they can say they love each other but be quite unaware of the negative emotional action which passes between them. They may be very "religious", they may say their prayers daily; they may visit the sick; they may be sincerely engaged in good works – and yet they may be emotionally extremely cruel to each other. The husband may crush the wife's potential for thought and creativity, and the wife strangle her husband's innate capacity to become an outstanding economist. You may think I am talking of rare cases, but from my studies I would estimate that 80 per cent of you here are engaged in such emotionally destructive activity, and you will not know about it. In fact, I would go so far as to say that some of you will be engaged in these "religious activities" in order to hide from yourselves the emotionally destructive things you are doing in your most intimate bonds and relationships. You go out to do good works, but with your wife, husband, children and parents you do destructive things to them emotionally.

'Ladies and gentlemen, the very place where your religion is most necessary is the place where it is lacking. It is what we do to each other emotionally that determines how we treat our neighbour, how we treat one another. What we do emotionally *is* our treatment of each other. Outwardly I may treat someone with politeness, but emotionally my actions betray the fact that he is in my mind a piece of rubbish. If someone was able to chart all my emotional actions towards a particular person but was unable to see the object towards which my actions tended, he would say the object must be a piece of rubbish or even a bit of shit. My dominant attitude then is one of contempt. In contempt I turn my back on the other with disgust, with a sneer: "Sweep this foul creature out of my way", I say. I turn my back. All this is external language to denote the emotional action whereby I negate my connection to the other.

'So, all who are Jews here: when you go into your homes to celebrate the Seder, if you are wounded and in pain, and turn your back upon its source, and turn to your rituals for escape, for comfort, while turning your back on the object which caused you the pain – then you perform an empty ritual. Go back to the source of pain, and confront it until you have come to terms with it.

'You Christians, as you go to your churches to celebrate the Eucharist and meditate on God's holy word, if you do this because you are disappointed in the responses of those close to you, it would be better that you cease going to your churches and face with courage the human disappointment in which you are involved. That is the place of your spiritual battle. The devil you have to wrestle with is in yourself, in your neighbour – not out in the wilderness, not apart from men.

'You Muslims, as you go to your mosque on Friday and lie prostrate before the mihrab, if your spouse is wounded by you, resents you, acts spitefully towards you it means you have committed emotional actions that have fostered this. Get up quickly, leave the mosque, and repair the damage.

'You Hindu, meditating on the Upanishads and practising a severe fast: your five-week-old child is missing you. He feels an absence. You are letting him down; go and attend to him and give up your ascesis and your meditation.

'You Buddhist, while begging with all humility with your bowl, you have left an embittered wife behind. Return and meet her; face her; do not run from her taunts. When you run away you embrace Mara and become his slave. When you face the accusations, process them, accept those that are true and repudiate those that are not, then you conquer Mara.

'All of you here: your spiritual struggle is no longer away in the desert, away in a silent retreat; it is the opposite: it is in the close bonds that the great emotional storms occur; it is here that the elemental struggle between good and evil takes place. By taking flight into your religious practices you escape the spiritual struggle.'

At this point a young lady stood up and said, 'But who are you? From where do you derive your knowledge?'

'I am a psychoanalyst' he replied.

'What sort of a person is that?' she asked.

'I am a person who studies the conflicts of the soul as they arise between two people intimately related, people with powerful emotional activity passing between them. I study this all day.'

'Then you are the person we need to teach us because we are going astray. This very conference is to discuss why all our religions have become irrelevant in the modern world. I think you have the key to our troubles', said the young woman, who had become their spokesperson.

I have stressed the existence of emotional action of which the individual is unaware, and yet its source is in the person. This means, therefore, that I am not aware that I am doing some of the things which I do; there is a part of my 'I' that I do not know. Psychoanalytic investigation reveals that there is frequently more than one part. The way I conceptualize it is that there are repositories within my 'I' for those actions of which I am unaware. To grasp what these repositories are, we need to reflect upon those actions of which we are unaware.

The core of our unawareness centres on actions which are damaging to the self and to others. It is these actions which I do not know about. They can be satisfactorily categorized according to the Seven Deadly Sins: pride, covetousness, lust, envy, gluttony, anger and sloth. There are, however, others which would be more germane to Eastern culture, for instance ignorance, which was emphasized by the Buddha and his followers.

When we see someone eating greedily or being greedy for money, this is an external manifestation of emotional greed. An analyst made an interpretation which made sense of a pattern of phenomena for his patient. She immediately wanted his ability to make such interpretations herself, becoming so preoccupied with wanting what he had that she was unable to take in the interpretation. It also became clear that this happened mentally within herself: when she generated some understanding, there was another part of her which quickly grabbed at the understanding and devoured it, perverting the understanding. The part of her which grabbed at the understanding and perverted it is the greedy part. There are also other parts inhabiting the personality: an envious part, a lazy part, a lustful part, and so on. These parts, each in their own way, interfere with the process of emotional integration and understanding.

So what we refer to as the subject is made up of many different agents. It is a psychological principle that only one agent can act at any one time, but over the course of a few minutes, even seconds, the agent principle can shift from one part to another. This shifting is difficult to detect in ordinary social intercourse, but can be witnessed by a psychoanalyst who is trained to observe such changes. These different parts of the self act against the activity of the self. This self is to be understood in the sense in which we have defined it from our examination of the Upanishads.

I have so far stressed that these parts of the self of which the individual has no conscious knowledge are attacking or self-destructive. However, the positive constructive emotion is muffled by the negative parts so that it does not find expression. The positive potential is strangled by the presence of these personalities that are not known. Therefore, the individual is unaware not only of the negative emotional action but also of the positive constructive emotion. Negative emotional action is doubly destructive: the individual is blocked from knowing those positive emotions within.

That which is known within but the consciousness of which cannot be borne is perceived in the outer forum. In the psychoanalytic situation, the negative emotional action and the positive constructive emotion are displaced onto the person of the analyst. If emotionally I act greedily but do not know it, then I perceive my analyst to be greedy. It is the emotional activity of which I am not conscious that is transferred on to the analyst. Thus these imagos of the analyst represent disowned parts of the self. The interpersonal, then, is symbolical of the intrapsychic.

The feelings experienced by the analyst but aroused by the patient constitute the counter-transference. Feelings, being the register of emotional action, are studied by the analyst in order to gain information about the emotional action-pattern in the patient. With fine tuning he will be able to differentiate between negative emotional action and positive constructive emotion. He will be able to infer the intrapsychic activity by what is being done to himself.

Self-knowledge is arrived at, then, through an interpersonal emotional encounter of great intimacy.

REFERENCE

John Macmurray (1936) *The Structure of Religious Experience* (London: Faber & Faber), p. 36.

18

Conscience and the Super-Ego

Dorothea's voice gave loud emphatic iteration to those muffled suggestions of consciousness which it was possible to explain as mere fancy, the illusion of exaggerated sensitiveness: always when such suggestions are unmistakably repeated from without, they are resisted as cruel and unjust. We are angered even by the full acceptance of our humiliating confessions – how much more by hearing in hard distinct syllables from the lips of a near observer, those confused murmurs which we try to call morbid, and strive against as if they were the oncoming of numbness! And this cruel outward accuser was there in the shape of a wife – nay, of a young bride, who, instead of observing his abundant pen scratches and amplitude of paper with the uncritical awe of an elegant-minded canary-bird, seemed to present herself as a spy watching everything with a malign power of inference.

(George Eliot, 1973)

I was once told the following story:

> Mother was sitting at her desk and could see the dining-room table on which there was a bowl of fruit. She saw her six-year-old son tip-toe in and take an apple from the bowl and then slip out again. Mother had asked her children not to take food between meals without asking her, so she made a mental note to speak to her son afterwards. Five minutes later, her son crept back and returned the apple to the bowl. As he did so, she heard him say, 'I've tricked the devil again.'

The boy wanted an apple. He had seen it in the bowl and there was no one around, he thought, so he would take it and eat it. What was it that prompted him to return the apple? One answer is fear of punishment, but his statement, 'I've tricked the devil again' does not suggest this; it suggests an internal reason. Let us suppose that fear of being found out was not the prime motive for returning the apple; that, as far as he knew, his theft of the apple had been entirely successful; that on the basis of the pleasure/pain principle there was nothing in the way of his eating the apple. What

154

reason could there be for him to return the apple? Something started to trouble him. The name we give this something is conscience.

When conscience speaks, it does not tell the boy he will be found out or punished. Conscience is a state of unease, but what is its rationale? Why not steal the apple? It makes no sense not to. If he has to lie to his mother, what does it matter? If I wish to murder or commit adultery and I can do so without being found out, then what sensible reason can there be for me not to do so? And if I lie and deceive in order to carry out my purposes, what reason can there be to deter me?

One social contract theory states that when human beings contract to live in society together they do so according to a code for the mutual advantage of all. When I cheat on my contractual obligations I experience this inner unease which we call conscience. A Christian view is that conscience is the voice of God speaking to the soul. Either way, I am dissuaded from satisfying my immediate desires on the basis of a higher principle.

If I satisfy my immediate sensual needs, then I act in accordance with the dictates of my erotic self. If it gives me pleasure to see someone squirm with embarrassment and I duly satisfy that desire, then my erotic self is the object to which I minister. If, however, I act according to conscience, then there is another self within me to which I do homage. The difference between the self guided by conscience and the erotic self is that the latter is myself with the other shut out. When I listen to my conscience I am attentive to a principle within me but which at the same time extends beyond me. It is *in* me but it is not *just* me; something has a claim on me which is at the same time greater than me.

It is difficult to avoid the conclusion that conscience speaks for that reality whose praises were sung by the seers who wrote the Upanishads. The seers comprehended this reality and meditated upon it. I believe, however, that it took the Buddha to realize that conscience was the manifestation of this reality. The Buddha stressed meditation just as did the seers of the Upanishads, but his realization that conscience was the organ of this reality gave his truth a practical application which had been lacking in a defined way within Hinduism. This realization was one of the great milestones in the religious story of mankind. For Socrates the pursuit of the good was *the* goal for the human being; it was to be chosen in preference to the dictates of the gods. However, Socrates did not unify the pursuit of the good with the comprehension of reality as did the Buddha. To act according to conscience is to pursue the good. The apprehension of the truth is through an act of the intellect. The pursuit of the good is through moral action. When the truth and the good are understood to coincide we have religion.

Contrary to common opinion, the super-ego is not synonymous with conscience. When Freud first introduced the term in 1923, he described it as a split-off part of the ego which stands above the ego, observing it. Later he came to see it as the seat of destructive forces. When Freud formulated the negative therapeutic reaction he saw the source of this to be in the super-ego. When a patient makes an emotional step forward, it is often followed by a sudden, sabotaging attack upon this new developmental gain. This attack, which can be extremely severe, is what is known as the negative therapeutic reaction, and the source of it is described as being in that part of the personality which Freud named the super-ego. I want to posit that when there is a savage super-ego operating, it means there is an activity going on of which the individual is extremely guilty.

I have outlined ways in which the individual acts emotionally against himself and also against others, especially those with whom he is intimate. However, this is not the way in which the matter is perceived by the man in the street. The person who is under the dominance of a savage super-ego may be extremely shy or very inhibited; a woman with a savage super-ego may be married to an authoritarian, bullying man.

The savage super-ego is an internal object, a part of the self that suffocates the real self, but this is not the way it is experienced. Instead, the individual finds him- or herself dominated by a tyrant *outside* and feels persecuted by that person. There are many other manifestations of super-ego activity: a person may look out very negatively upon the world, have no confidence or trust, always believe things will work out badly, or talk of himself disparagingly. Sometimes the latter is projected outwards so that friends are spoken of in a very disparaging manner. The activity of the super-ego colours the mentality of the person in question so that it looks as though the person is the victim of outer events – however, psychoanalysis reveals that the situation is quite unlike what it appears.

The savage super-ego is reproaching the ego for something. What emerges from psychoanalytic investigation is that the savage attacks of the super-ego are always present where the other as a feeling person is obliterated. I will give an example. A man would drink heavily while at work, then go to his club and play bridge. Frequently he would forget that his wife had arranged a dinner party, and so would arrive back as the guests were leaving. When his wife shouted at him, he thought her utterly unreasonable. He could only see things from his point of view: after a hard day at the office he needed a few drinks to relax, and he got home in a much better temper when he had had a few rounds of bridge at his club. This man was also in analysis. He expected his analyst to give him times to suit him; he would come into sessions and start rapidly talking. When the analyst made an interpretation, he would say, 'How very interesting' and quickly go on talking. If he did hear the analyst, he would have forgotten what had been said by the next session. He only remembered what he himself had said.

The analyst as a separate person did not exist for the man, who felt persecuted by his wife. The analyst did not make any comments about the man's blindness to his wife's distress because he believed it would have no effect. Instead, he tried another method which proved to be more effective. When he made an interpretation and the man said, 'How interesting' and went on talking, the analyst pointed out that he had not attended to what the analyst had said but with the 'How interesting' remark had just brushed it aside. He also worked upon the way in which the man's memory had erased any realization which had occurred in the previous session.

The analyst worked upon all the manoeuvres by which the patient obliterated the analyst's presence for a period of three years. At the end of that time the patient reported the following changes: he felt more warmly towards his wife, it was rare for him to go to his club to play bridge after work, and he drank much less. He had received a promotion at work because of the foreign contracts which he had pulled off for the company. He said that he believed he was a competent businessman, whereas before he had denigrated himself. Then, after two and a half years, he suddenly wondered in a session whether his analyst had a wife. Such a question had never occurred to him before – he had not thought of his analyst as a person who might be married. As he became more thoughtful of the other, as the other began to have affective existence, so did his super-ego diminish and concurrently he began to develop a functioning conscience. The super-ego was admonishing the man for his emotional abolition of the other.

Therefore, we are saying that the savage super-ego is a component part of the narcissistic personality structure, whereas a functioning conscience is an essential part of a healthy, outgoing personality. Conscience is the foundation stone of natural mature religion.

It is only when the super-ego begins to diminish in the intensity of its activity that it begins to be replaced by conscience. It is a fact that the super-ego banishes conscience. We may remember that conscience is the manifestation of reality in me. So the emotional presence of the other and

157

the presence within me of reality are one and the same thing. When the other is obliterated, so also is reality, and therefore conscience is rubbed out also. This means that the super-ego is part of the erotic self.

Erotic craving also muffles conscience; it is for this reason that spiritual leaders have taught that it is necessary not to be led by erotic craving, which is what the Buddha meant by being in a state free from desire. The super-ego condemns, but in the very condemnation the individual stays stuck in the erotic craving. This craving is not only for food, drink or sex, but also craving to be loved, to be admired; it is also craving for power, position or status. These latter desires are always accompanied by alluring erotic fantasies. The super-ego says to the ego, 'You are wicked', but in its very revulsion reveals a negative attraction. The origin of the super-ego lies in a sensual revulsion. The super-ego allows for no distinctions; it coalesces disparate elements into one condemned entity. What is most important in terms of our enquiry is that it stifles the voice of conscience. So when the clinician meets a savage super-ego he will know that conscience is not functioning in the patient, that the other exists in an obliterated state, and that there is emotional activity that maintains this state of affairs. In order to reverse this situation, the clinician will have to draw the patient's attention to this activity of which he is unaware and slowly allow the presence of the other to come into relation to the ego, thereby restoring the function of conscience.

Conscience is the foundation stone of natural religion. It is the echo in the ego of reality, of the other. I do not have to follow the suggestions of conscience. If I do so it cannot be explained on the basis of efficient causes, but because I choose to do so. Conscience, then, is a final cause; it operates at a different level of causality from that of the pleasure/pain principle. I do not follow conscience through being driven; I choose against pressure. I cannot say the reason why I choose. When I choose to follow conscience it brings me into relation with an object. It may not bring me material advantage. There is no reason of a practical nature that I can use to urge the following of conscience.

Let us go back to the example given at the beginning of the chapter. When the boy decides to return the apple rather than steal it, he feels differently from if he had stolen it. Each of the alternative actions produces a different registration of feeling in the boy. If he perseveres in stealing the apple he feels bad, if he decides to return it and not steal he feels good. In the former action he has muffled reality; in the latter he has attended to reality. In the former he has neglected himself; in the latter he has cared for himself, but in the latter action his mother is included in this attention and care.

This last fact has a very important effect: the boy's mother is affected by the boy's action – it is an action which touches her. You may say that the mother cannot be affected by an action which she does not see. In fact, in the example I have given the mother did see and was affected. She felt a warm love for her son. Even had she not physically seen her son return the apple she would have *felt* the action and so had a warm love for him. She acts warmly towards him because he had cared for her reality as well as his. She acts warmly towards him not because she wants to, but because she has love for him. She acts freely.

I had a patient once whose boss, whom I shall call Mr Smith, exploited her. He expected her to work during her lunch hour; he kept her back dictating letters after hours; he never offered her extra money; he treated her as an inferior object, and he expected her to do humiliating things for him. Once, he demanded that she carry into his office a soaking, soggy carpet which was in the boot of his car and she got her skirt and blouse wet and dirty.

When she came into the consulting-room for a session, she scowled as if she were walking past a smelly rubbish dump: when I made an interpretation, she would act as if I had not spoken. Just as she said she was exploited by Mr Smith at work, so in a similar way I felt exploited by her, treated as a bit of rubbish fit only for the garbage bin. I had pointed this out to her but to no effect, when one day I marshalled my evidence more efficiently and placed it all before her. She paused and I felt certain she had taken it in. When she came in the next day, she told me that, surprisingly, Mr Smith had treated her quite differently from ever before. For example, he had looked at his watch just before one o'clock and said, 'Oh, it's lunch-time. Make sure that you get your lunch!', and in the evening when he was dictating letters he saw that it was 5.30 and he had said to her, 'Oh, it's half past five. I'll keep the rest of these letters until tomorrow', and he had smiled warmly at her when she left the office to go home. The woman's boss had behaved benignly towards her because her emotional activity towards him had changed, and therefore he was responding differently. However, she herself was quite unaware that she was acting differently, and Mr Smith's behaviour came as a complete surprise to her. I will now explain how I think this came about.

I posit that the woman acted emotionally in a new way towards Mr Smith, because of what I had said to her the previous day and her reception of it. Below the threshold of awareness, she 'saw' her activity when I spoke to her that day. In that act of 'seeing', she could do the activity no longer. This is based on the Socratic principle that she could not know she was doing bad and also do it. So the act of seeing was itself a turning point: seeing is deciding. Why was it that she saw her activity on that day but not before? I think the only possible answer to that question is that she was able to, partly because I had applied my comments on that day with emotional conviction. This leads to a further question: why did I apply my comments with emotional conviction on that day, whereas I had not before? Because I saw matters with greater clarity. But how did that happen? It suggests there was a change in me and a change in her, and that this change was in the direction of greater responsiveness to that reality in which she and I shared, and that this reality was speaking to me as well as to her. It led to a virtuous act on my part and on her part. This call of reality requires emotional strength to hearken to and act upon. It requires the individual to break through the power of what is known as projective identification.

Projective identification is that activity that muffles freedom of action, muffles conscience, and strangles free communication in the other. Mr Smith, we suppose, acted warmly towards my patient on the next day because he wanted to – he was not pressured into doing so. I am in the grip of projective identification when I am pressured into acting in a particular way against my own inner desires. Such pressure is extremely powerful; the source of such pressure comes from the super-ego.

There are these two sources of action within the mind: conscience and the super-ego. When I am under the power of the super-ego I *have* to have a drink or fast; have a holiday or work fifteen hours a day; get up and clamour at a meeting or keep quiet as a mouse. I want to ask my uncle a favour but when I am in his presence I just can't; I have to have beer before I can start work. I have to have read all the books on the reading list before I can start my essay; I have to answer my letter from Aunt Mary before going to lunch although I keep everyone else waiting. All these activities find their source in the super-ego. If someone asks me, 'But *why* do you have to have a drink?', I have no answer. The answer is I have to because I have to; I must because I must. I may give some answers but they do not carry conviction; they are rationalizations, which means they are pretend reasons. Actions which find their origin in the super-ego have no thought in them – they are devoid of scientific content. Therefore the cult, ceremony and ritual of primitive religion finds its origin in the super-ego. If you ask one of the Dinka, 'Why do you offer this goat in sacrifice? Why do you believe it will ward off a storm?', he will have no rational answer to give you.

Actions whose source are in the super-ego are closely linked to instinct. They are not totally instinct-bound, but they are close to it. We have defined instinct as group-driven behaviour. The super-ego is the inheritance in the individual of this group-driven behaviour, from which there has been only the beginning of intentional action. The group has to discipline the individual truant through sanctions – usually through group exclusion.

When I follow conscience, however, the psychological process is quite different. In this case when I act I *want* to act; I act out of my own freedom. It seems a paradox that I am beckoned by conscience but that when I follow it I act freely. The only hypothesis that makes sense of this is that conscience is the manifestation of my deepest reality, and therefore I act from what is most truly me. Yet this deep reality in me is shared; there is reality in which I and the other participate. There is another important element to this. I follow conscience, and when someone asks me why I did this action rather than another, I am able to give an answer informed by thought. Three elements are held in close thrall: I act according to conscience; I think and I act from love rather than fear. The latter is the beginning of mature religion; thinking is the beginning of scientific enquiry. The conclusion confronts us that science and mature religion originate in the same process of psychological individuation. It is surprising to realize that true thought, as opposed to mimetic parroting, cannot occur without a grounding in free action and conscience.

The pursuit of conscience is the beginning of natural religion and also the foundation stone of mature religion. The link between the pursuit of conscience and thought and our deeper reality is in knowledge. Actions that flow from this source are known; actions that flow from the super-ego are felt. I smoke heavily and I know that it aggravates my bronchitis; I feel uneasy and my conscience pricks me; I also know that it causes me to cough at night which keeps my wife awake. After some deliberation I give up smoking; I know that it is a good thing and I feel healthier and more content. These latter feelings have a foundation in knowledge.

When I am driven by the super-ego I feel sorry for myself, which is not built upon knowledge but upon false perception or false reasoning. I am talking to my analyst, and in mid-sentence he announces that it is time to end. I am hurt and wounded and I think to myself, 'How cruel he is to cut me off so rudely and abruptly.' The next day I am due to catch the train and my wife says to me 'Darling, couldn't you just fix the light in the cooker hood before you go?' So I do it. However, I miss my train and catch the next one, so I am a quarter of an hour late for my session the next day. Now my analyst says to me, 'I think that when I interrupted you in mid-sentence yesterday you felt I was savage and unfeeling.' I remember how I had said to myself, 'God, you are cruel', so I tell my analyst that he is right, and that I had said to myself how cruel he was.

My analyst points out that I often start talking rapidly just as the session is coming to an end, and I thought it was reasonable from his point of view that he take the matter in hand. This means that my judgement, 'God, you are cruel' is not right. Who was speaking in me when I made that judgement? It was a grandiose me – 'How dare he interrupt me when I am talking?' The 'great me' has been treated with dishonour. If in sober judgement, in the light of hindsight, I recognize that my analyst was not cruel, then how come I felt sorry for myself? It can only be that I was cruel to myself. When I was treated so dishonourably by my analyst I said to myself, 'To hell with him', and I turned inwardly against him – but also against my rational self, my inner reality. I no longer had my own reality to guide me. I had become an emotional victim, and this is why I felt sorry for myself. In that state I also had become victim to my wife's request, which she would not even have made had I not already psychologically mutilated myself. Now we come to the important part. When I mutilate myself, when I turn against my own inner reality, when I turn against my analyst I am acting very savagely. The source of this savage action against myself is the super-ego. I have a sadistic tyrant within which is a facet of the 'great me'. I cannot bear to know that I am so savage, that I can act so savagely, so I project it outwards on to my analyst. Therefore the psychological process is quite different. In this case I feel sorry for myself, I misperceive the agent of cruelty, and am devoid of knowledge. This is the situation when the super-ego is in control; it is radically different from action flowing from the beckoning of conscience.

The super-ego and conscience exist in inverse ratio to each other. This may become clear if we return to the above example. When my wife asks me to fix her cooker hood, I hear it as a command: I am being told to do this. I am in this state because I have savagely attacked myself; at this level conscience is no longer operating, so the super-ego takes over. I turn up a quarter of an hour late for my analytic session the following day. I am in antagonism to my own self and to my analyst but I do not know it. I have acted against conscience – savagely, mutilating myself, and the super-ego takes power. As conscience begins to reassert itself so the power of the super-ego diminishes. The analyst pointed out to me what had occurred, and when I acknowledged my 'God-you-are-cruel' thought, a channel of communication opened up between me and my analyst. Reasoning began to assert itself, so the power of the super-ego diminished.

So also do primitive and mature religion exist in inverse ratio to each other, Mature religion replaces primitive religion, and as the mentality of primitive religion expands, so the power of mature religion diminishes.

When I am operating under the direction of the super-ego, I find it unbearable to know I have this inside me and am acting according to its principles and so I take flight. But to what do I take flight? Into ritual, dogmatic thinking, rationalizations, lust, drunkenness, drug-taking and greed. All these, even ritual and dogmatic thinking, are supported by sensual gratification: the 'great me' is gratified. I live at a surface level where I abort mental life and the truth and the good.

The emotional sphere is the most important place where these two sources of action operate. The activities in this sphere are frequently below the threshold of awareness. When I was 'obeying' my wife's injunction to repair the cooker hood, I had no knowledge of the savage way in which I had mutilated my inner reality. What psychoanalysis reveals is the operation of these emotional activities that occur intrapsychically and interpersonally.

It may seem a contradiction to say that I can have knowledge and yet be unaware of it. Yet when the analyst explained what I had done, I saw the truth of it. This implies that what the analyst says touches something that I know. It is because of the savage mutilator of inner reality and conscience that I turn my back on what I know. This ability of the human being to turn aside from inner horror, and so split himself in two, is the mechanism through which the unconscious is fashioned. The undoing of this construction is the work of psychoanalysis. In the sphere of emotional intimacy psychoanalysis has as its goal the transformation of primitive religious mentality into mature religion. This is a very burdensome work because it requires the analysand to recognize his savagery towards himself and others – usually towards those who are closest to him.

REFERENCE

George Eliot (1973) *Middlemarch* (Harmondsworth: Penguin Books), pp. 232–3.

19

Self-Knowledge, Virtue and Mental Health

Kitty made the acquaintance of Madame Stahl, too, and this acquaintance, together with her friendship with Varenka, not only had a great influence on her, it was also a comfort in her mental distress. She found this comfort through a completely new world being opened to her by means of this acquaintance, a world that had nothing in common with her past, an exalted, noble world, from the heights of which she could contemplate her past calmly. It was revealed to her that besides the instinctive life to which she had given herself up hitherto there was a spiritual life. This life was disclosed in religion but a religion having nothing in common with the religion Kitty had known since childhood . . . .

(Tolstoy, 1986)

The thesis of this chapter is that self-knowledge is achieved in direct ratio to the degree to which a person acquires virtue. 'Acquisition of virtue' suggests that it is possible to build up capital in the personality, that by doing something the person lays down a deposit from which he is able subsequently to draw. How are we to understand this notion of a 'deposit' in the personality? It has to mean that a psychic action creates something. We have then to ask what does it create, and out of what?

On the assumption that I do not create out of nothing, what is the raw material that I act upon? What is the something out of which I create? What is our fundamental psychic matter? If we say it is a bundle of instincts, this suggests they have a neutral value, which does not seem to be the case. The evidence seems to be that psychic matter is an energy, which if not chosen against is negative. Therefore, the material out of which we act creatively is a negative one. But what is this 'material' in the personality? It is something that carries the 'I' along like a piece of driftwood in a current. It is the energy whose source is in the instincts.

When I say 'I *shall* not choose', in this refusal lies the source of all trouble, because when it is chosen either for or against it becomes a capital deposit in the personality. So it is an energy whose quality is dependent upon this choice; it is turned bad or good according to refusal or acceptance – it is a nameless energy. Is the word 'drive' or 'instinct' better?

Strachey translated Freud's word *Triebe* as 'instinct', though many today think 'drive' is better. I think it better to conceptualize what this energy is and then to name it, rather than get bogged down as to whether Freud's meaning has been correctly translated. After all, Freud may not have named it for the best.

We have said that it is an energy whose source is in the group. This is different from Freud's formulation, which was that the source was in the body. In this group-tied energy, we are bound by the aim of group- and self-preservation. For this reason I prefer the word 'instinct' as it contains within it the concept of aim. However, it does not contain the sense that an unchosen something in the personality acts negatively. It would mean that the instinct is negative. Are we here into the riddle of the death instinct? A negative force in the personality? It seems clear that 'instinct' is not the right word because it is negative, because of its 'unchosenness'. It was right to name it instinct prior to the burial climax but not after. It becomes a negative force because of its unchosenness. It is the capacity to choose which has changed us from being instinct-driven animals into humans. So 'instinct' is no longer the right word. We are talking now of a negative force which results from unchosenness. What are we to call it? Because it is unchosen it is anti-human. I propose to call it then the 'anti-human force' in the personality.

The choice converts anti-human force into a capital deposit in the individual. The anti-human force is a detritus in the personality, carrying the individual further and further into degradation, like Macbeth. On the other hand, a choice, which is always choice for and choice against, constitutes something in the personality. The question is obvious that in virtue there is a choice and therefore something is opted for. When we try to understand what this is, the only thing we can come up with is that we choose what is. Clinical observation can help us to realize that I choose to own what is me. The very act by which I choose that which is me alters the character of the me that I am. I shall illustrate this.

My wife telephones home and speaks to her mother and father twice a week. Something strange occurs because I do not know it although I am in the same room when she telephones. When I see her on the telephone I believe that she is talking to our dog, and that the telephone is a bone which she is offering to the dog. A friend comes in and I tell him that my wife has got a bone in her hand and is talking to our dog, about to offer the dog this bone. The friend notices that I seem very agitated. He gets so worried that he arranges for me to visit a psychoanalyst. The analyst points out that I am so jealous of my wife's relations with her parents that I disown it and make what I see into something else: I make the telephone into a bone; it looks similar and sounds similar. When the analyst says this I own this intensely jealous part of myself, and the jealousy decreases. I am now able to see that the instrument that my wife is holding is a telephone. (I need to point out that it takes five years of analysis for me to come to own this part of myself. It is not magic.)

The act of virtue is taking possession of what is me. This possession of myself which comes about through choice is the act of virtue. The word 'virtue' comes from the Latin *virtus* meaning strength. It takes strength to make this act of self-possession. The only way to conceptualize this is with a ground-plan where the personality is constructed out of parts.

The anti-human force exists in parts in a personalized form. Some Kleinian clinicians have named these parts 'the gang' or 'the mafia'. This designation is a good one because these parts are neither fully personal nor just a force. This is consistent with my definition of instinct as a group-bound energy. The anti-human force is not personalized but 'group-ized' – it has a group form within the personality. The group does not think, only the individual thinks. The group has a personality form, however, which is in opposition to the individual thinker. It is the presence in the personality of our pre-Axial Era tribal past. These group personalities have voices and they use arguments, but they do not think. They are against individual creation because they have not been chosen or owned.

These group personalities can be conceptualized according to the traditional Christian vices: a greedy personality, an envious personality, a jealous personality, a cruel personality. (For the sake of brevity I shall use the adjective 'vicious' to be inclusive of the greedy, envious, jealous and cruel for the rest of this chapter.) This conceptualization plays a big part in the clinical interpretations of analysts of the Kleinian school. The intense activity of these personalities is directed against the ego, which is weakened thereby. In its state of weakness the ego has then to find a means by which to manage its way in the world. It does this by burying itself in an ecstatic object.

Such an object either enjoys an independent existence outside of the self, or it is generated within by the self. In either case the ego generates its own sensuous excitement in which the ego loses itself. It is a quality of the ecstatic object that the ego believes itself to be good because it is dissociated from the bad. This occurs because the ego is split and buried in the vicious personalities and the ecstatic object. I suggest two examples of this. First, a man fell in love with a woman of great beauty. He was entranced by her and married her. He remained enraptured until her tummy swelled up with a baby, when the trance broke and he became full of rage. Second, a woman convert to Catholicism had great devotion to God, to Jesus, to the

Virgin Mary, and attended all church services with great fervour. Then she developed cancer and on her death-bed she cursed God and the church for having betrayed her.

Being buried in an ecstatic object is correlated with being buried in the vicious personalities. Burial *in* is an action of the 'I'. Burial in the ecstatic object protects the ego from knowledge of its activity in the vicious personalities. The 'I' cannot be 'in' and know because knowledge is a function of having a part that is not in. Not to be in means not to act; I am in through acting. Therefore, when I cease to act in there is access to knowledge. Acting in the vicious personalities means I am acting viciously but do not know it because I am acting in and through the ecstatic object. One part of my ego is acting in the ecstatic object and the rest is acting in the vicious personalities. The part that needs to be independent in order to have knowledge is buried in the ecstatic object and is passive.

Knowledge is the product of split parts of the ego joining up. The junction of parts comes about through action. The ego's action clearly is to extricate itself from being in the ecstatic object and in the vicious personalities. The question is, how does it do this if it is split? How can it be the source of such an action when, by being split, this is prevented? The answer is that there is a relatedness between split parts of the ego and such action is possible but very much restricted. It is like a blob of water that disperses into droplets whose watery nature yet always inclines them to join up. Initiatory action is the ego's nature. Being split reduces the potential strength of initiatory action, but does not annihilate it altogether.

There is an activity keeping the split parts separate, the source of which is in the vicious personalities. These hold ego-parts captive and use them for their own purposes – against the ego's own self. The definition of the vicious personalities is that they are against the ego, against the self.

The virtuous act is an action of the ego which frees split parts from captivity, from being agents of the vicious personalities, and brings them into unity. It is an act of strength, and the action itself integrates. For this to be possible, ego-parts must join in making an option which is for and not against itself. The virtuous act is an act which frees ego-parts from the imprisonment of the vicious personalities.

The social environment favours either the persistence of the against-self – the ego's activities within the vicious personalities – or it disfavours them. The vicious personalities are only able to continue functioning by approval or stroking from figures in the external environment. They are like boa-constrictors that wrap themselves around an external figure, which gives an impetus, a thrust to the vicious activity. The vicious personalities need this thrill to keep going. If the social environment declines to go along with the enticements of the vicious personalities, they are deprived of their strength, of their fuel. At the same time, conscience makes itself heard. It is the voice beckoning the virtuous act, reproaching the vicious act. The virtuous act integrates the ego-parts. A product of integration of the ego-parts is knowledge; therefore the virtuous act is the prerequisite for self-knowledge. Self-knowledge and virtue therefore are partners to one another.

I want now to look at this in the way it is experienced in psychoanalysis. It is a common clinical experience for a patient to realize he is jealous at a point when he is less jealous than previously. In other words, he realizes that he is jealous subsequent to an act of virtue. When he is acting 'in' the jealous personality he does not know it.

A patient would come into the consulting-room at a rush and immediately start speaking. She would invariably arrive late, never use the waiting-room, and then rush out a couple of minutes before time. She would speak very hurriedly. In the early part of the treatment she sat in a chair and eyed me closely. I noticed that when my eyes wandered out of the window or away from her, her voice faltered and she gave up what she was saying. After four years of treatment, she one day got a glimpse of this and said, 'Maybe I don't use the waiting-room in order to avoid seeing any of your other patients.' The next day she had a dream in which she was with her mother attending the funeral of her sister. Her father was not present. She understood this to be a representation of her jealous desire to have mother to herself. The dream came at a time when she was not fully in the jealous personality. At the same time, she began to use the waiting-room and stay until the end of the sessions. The dream is a primitive thought. She now thinks it because she is not in it. The fact that she is not in it, whereas she was, indicates that an action has taken place – an action which freed her.

It is revealing to examine the conditions that favoured this inner action. In clinical psychoanalysis, the patient as boa-constrictor tries to enwrap the analyst and thereby provide the thrill, the fuel, to keep the vicious personalities in existence. It is the analyst's job to repudiate this role. The constant application of this role slowly deprives the patient of this source of action. A new solution has to be found and the patient is forced back upon his or her own ego-strengths. This procedure favours the act of freedom, which is the virtuous act. This act consolidates the ego and brings with it new knowledge. The psychoanalytic environment is one that favours the virtuous act.

In Chapter 6 I stated that spirituality consists of a state established by good actions which transcend the dictates of the survival instinct. The meaning of virtuous acts as described here conforms to the definition of the spiritual. If it is accurate to say that the goal of psychoanalysis is self-knowledge, and if our argument is right that self-knowledge is dependent upon the virtuous act, then the process of psychoanalysis is a spirituality.

Frequently psychoanalysis occurs without patients acquiring self-knowledge; frequently it is conducted by analysts without self-knowledge. This means that we have the external 'cultus' without the corresponding inner acts. We are forced to conclude that psychoanalysis is a religion as well as a spirituality. The external cultus consists in the defined setting of analyst, patient, the use of the couch, the fifty-minute session five days a week, and so on. This is the religious cultus. The spiritual depends upon the inner act of virtue.

The act of virtue is taken against the force of the vicious personalities. It is an act of daring. It is just such an attitude to life that constitutes the basis for mental health; the act of virtue establishes the foundations for mental health.

Life is beset with crises. These crises, real or imagined, confront us along life's journey. The most unavoidable crisis is our own death. There are many other crises. In childhood it would be the death of our mother or father, the birth of a brother or sister. The crises can be divided into two categories: those that happen to us, and those that we are instrumental in bringing about. Some disasters, like the death of a parent, happen to us; others we bring on our own heads, like failing an exam because we have not bothered to study. It is those that are fashioned by our own mistakes that carry on throughout life.

We have crises, whoever has fashioned them. Mental health or ill-health is defined according to our attitude to these facts. Our mental attitude towards an event alters the event. It is part of the event. A change in mental attitude therefore changes the event. There is a wide spectrum of mental attitudes to events. There are two basic mental attitudes on which all the others are constructed: facing the event, or taking flight from it. When something is terribly sad, I can turn my back upon it, flee from it, or face it – in fact, embrace it.

I can take flight from the event in various ways. The outer event is also an inner event, so in order to take flight from an inner reality there are various courses open to me: I can cut myself in two and then disown the part that is in contact with the sadness; I can discharge the sadness into someone else and so disown it in myself; I can separate the knowledge from the affect and push the affect off onto something else. The destruction of inner reality involves an assault on the ego. The ego is split up and thereby impoverished. So I have to fashion a miracle ego – a Humpty-Dumpty that is miraculously put together. The miracle ego can then perform miraculous acts. It can get rid of sadness, transfer affect from one place to another, push the sadness into another. The miracle ego is a phantasy, however, because the reality is a fragmented and impoverished ego. The miracle ego is a make-believe into which I put the disowning part of myself, although the phantasy is that this is the whole me. The miracle ego performs miraculous acts, but these acts cover up the fundamental act, which is a disowning of the sadness.

Entering into relation with the sadness is the courageous act, the act of virtue. This is the precondition of being able to face life's crises. Mature mental health is that state of mind that enables a person to face life's crises – incorporate them, work through them, and be ready for the next phase of life. The capacity to manage an external crisis is consequent upon the ego's conquest of the vicious personalities within. The act of conquest, this act of strength *is* the act of virtue. Therefore mental health depends upon the act of virtue; it is the source of mental health.

REFERENCE

L. N. Tolstoy (1986) *Anna Karenin* (Harmondsworth: Penguin Books), p. 242.

20

Psychoanalysis – A Spirituality

It is only in our immediate intercourse with human beings that we have insight into the character of man. We must actually confront man, we must meet him squarely face to face, in order to understand him.

(Cassirer, 1972)

The purpose of detachment is to uncloak spiritual action in all its nakedness. For the mystic, it was only when this action was revealed that it was possible to distinguish good from bad. Mystics were men who had devoted themselves to this inner scrutiny with the goal of triumphing over the bad and establishing the good. The good was then an internal possession whose light they followed. They were thus able to abandon primitive religion, although they retained elements of the religious tradition in which they were socialized. So, for instance, the Buddha maintained the doctrine of reincarnation and built his theory of *karma* into it.

The internal possession of the good is what guided these mystics, who were also founders of the great religious traditions. They all founded institutions, which embodied the good in a scriptural canon whose function was to encapsulate the teachings of the founder. This was then entrusted to a responsible body whose job was to guard the doctrine. The moment the good is made incarnate in these two components the institution is born. This marks the transition from spirituality to religion.

A religion, then, is an institution whose goal is the good. The way the good is conceptualized differs in primitive religion and mature religion. In primitive religion the good is conceived to be the physical survival of the individual and the tribe; in mature religion it is the salvation of the individual members through meaning. In primitive religion the good is articulated through rites, ceremonies and mythology; in mature religion it is through a scriptural canon and an official body whose purpose it is to interpret the message of the founder faithfully to the people. Mature

171

religion always originates either in a single known founder such as the Buddha or Jesus, or through a series of teachers increasingly deeper in their spirituality, as in Judaism or Hinduism. In all these religions there is ultimately a canon which governs the pattern of all future development.

A person is religious who is a member of one of the known religions. This membership can be either explicit or implicit. In the case of the former, the individual participates in the rites and devotional life of the religion in an identifiable way. Most religions have ceremonies of initiation, or rites of passage. There are also implicit members who belong to a religion through affective sympathy: they do not hold to all the doctrines, do not attend the ceremonies regularly, but have either been initiated formally, or, at some point in their lives, through affective bonds.

However, such membership only exacts commitment at the level of words and sentiments. Adherence to the good can remain merely at the level of external attachment. Tartuffe of Molière's play characterizes a person who displays great religiosity in his expressed sentiments but whose behaviour is at variance with his external declarations. Prince Luzhin in Dostoievsky's *Crime and Punishment* displays similar hypocrisy. So it is possible to be religious but unspiritual.

A spiritual person is one who makes the good an internal possession. For an unknown reason, an individual gives priority in his life to the spiritual quest to discover the intentional base of his actions, to detach himself from those which are bad, and to pursue those which are good. It is possible for someone to be spiritual but not to belong explicitly to a religion. However, a spiritual person often belongs implicitly in his sympathies to one or more of the religious traditions.

The person who is in search of the motive that drives his actions in order to purify his intentions is engaged in spiritual activity. The mystic searches into himself, into the deepest layers of his being whence the power of action emanates. To determine the nature of this action requires reflection.

Intentional action has a psychic source and a psychic object. This can be translated as a spiritual source and a spiritual object. The object has no extension or colour and exists beyond time; it could be called a metaphysical object. The action is determined by the object and receives its structure from it. The object raises the source to its level. Insight into the nature of the action comes about through connaturality.

It is not quite so, however, that the action is determined by the object. Rather, it is that the source is *known* through the object: the object is the revealer of the source. The source of action cannot be directly known; it is the *noumenon*. The object can be known directly, and the active subject indirectly. The known object is the symbol through which the unknown subject is grasped. The action is connatural to the two. We do not have three entities but a single reality shared by all three. It is possible to make a logical separation but not a real one. We are looking at a red box. It is possible to separate the boxness from the redness logically but not really. Subject, object and action are three aspects of one reality.

In analysis we frequently come to a realization that what is said is not real. There is the implication that there is something real and something not real. For the ascetic, there is a detachment from the unreal and attachment to the real. It is this definition of the real that needs some investigation.

The basis upon which the real is separated from the unreal is axiological. That is, when you say that this is real and something else is not real, it is a value judgement. This is not so in the natural sciences, where the real and the unreal are distinguished on the basis of whether something exists or does not. A phoenix has no existence but a horse does. However, a phoenix has mental existence, so when it comes to the mind on what basis are we to make this distinction? I will use the example mentioned before.

A patient complains that her husband bullies her. The analyst has a mental hypothesis that this means that the patient is bullying the analyst, that this is unknown to the patient, and, until then, to the analyst. The analyst then remembers that he has been persuaded by the patient to believe that an interpretation he made was wrong. He is conscious that at the time he had not truly thought it was wrong; he had been persuaded against his own inner judgement. He then realizes that this has been a pattern.

Later in the session, when the patient tries again to persuade him that his interpretation of the previous day is not right, the analyst then challenges the patient. He points out that this happens again and again, and gives evidence that this is an attempt to persuade the analyst away from his own judgement; that she bullies him, in other words. The patient takes this in, and in the next session reports that she stood up to her husband and was not bullied by him. I will not go into how this came about, but will concentrate upon something else.

In the analyst's hypothesis there is a value judgement: it is bad to be bullied and good to refuse to be bullied. There is also another element. The analyst might agree with the patient and say, 'Yes, I understand that your husband is a bully. I am struck by the fact that it never occurs to you to leave him.' The analyst would be saying that it is not good to be bullied, and his value judgement would be that it is a good thing to leave the person who is bullying. I will refer to the two analysts as the Fight Analyst and the Flight Analyst. It needs to be emphasized that these two analysts are in agreement that it is a bad thing to be bullied. A Christian analyst, however, might say that to turn the other cheek is a good thing. The two analysts are in disagreement as to the mode of dealing with the bully. The Fight Analyst says it is a good thing to stand up to the bully, the Flight Analyst says the best course is to escape from the bully.

The crucial issue here is that the psychoanalyst believes that the good lies in directing attention towards the inner actions of different parts of the self. If it is asked why does the psychoanalyst do this, his answer is that he believes that the good lies in such an endeavour. If you asked a mystic why he directs his attention to inner action, he could only answer that this is his *daimon*. Following the example just given, the analyst might say that it brings about a better result: that if the patient's husband stops bullying her, it will make her life more comfortable; yet that is not correct as it is possible that the change in her might have enraged her husband even more. The psychoanalyst would say that what she had done was still right. It is an inherent belief of psychoanalysis that to own the different parts of ourselves is a good thing in itself. The Fight Analyst has said it is a good thing to stand up to the intrapsychic bully; it is a bad thing to identify the bully as a whole entity outside. An analysis in the view of the Fight Analyst is a process which assists the analysand to struggle against inner figures. Now we begin to get near our definition of the real.

In the clinical example there is real change. The patient is able emotionally not to be bullied. She repels the charge of the bully. She moves from a state where she invites in the bully to one where she repels it. When she invites in the bully, she consents to being pushed, to being controlled by another.

The 'management of inner figures' is a euphemism for the owning of a controlling part of the self, a greedy part of the self, an envious part of the self. When the individual angles his focus towards the management of inner figures, he constructs a bridge to this disowned part, in contrast to disowning a part of himself. It is the difference between these two action structures that separates the real from the unreal.

Every entity in the universe is in relation to every other entity. The same principle applies in the individual psychic world. There are two modes of relating: intentional and anti-intentional. In intentional relating there is a 'yes', in anti-intentional relating there is a 'no' to the psycho-ontological structure. The 'yes' that goes with the ontological structure is the real; it affirms reality. The 'no' that inwardly repudiates the structure is unreal.

There is then an intentional centre that goes with structure or against it. It is a source of action. Going with the structure, the source of action is active; going against the structure, the source is passive. In this case the source renounces its own nature. It is a paradox that in intentional relating the source is active when it goes with the structure; passive when it goes against the structure.

Is the individual inactive in anti-intentional relating? When he goes against structure it abjures its being because the intentional source receives its character from its place in the structure. Anti-intentional relating abjures its own being. In this case, then, what is the source of action in the personality? The anti-intentional act sets into motion an anti-structure.

The puzzle is the how of the anti-intentional act. We have in us this capacity to abjure our own being. This statement brings us into touch with those spiritual leaders who have significantly altered our value systems. They have proclaimed a message where they have stated 'This is our Being', 'This is man's nature', 'This is the Path to follow'. They have not abjured man's being; in their Enlightenment they have enlightened an essential aspect of man's being.

There is implied here that most of us are in darkness; that we do not know our own nature and in what direction to find fulfilment.

Anti-intentional acts keep us in darkness. It is for this reason that illumination is set in train by an intentional act, which occurs concurrently with detachment. The Buddha's supreme intentional act, his Enlightenment, occurred when he had detached himself from the ascetics in the Deer Park.

Anti-intentional acts attach to and intentional acts detach from. It is now a question of examining the way in which the anti-intentional act attaches, and to what it attaches. It is buried in the sensual, the material object. It does not stand on its own. Its anti-intentionality is a life refusal, and consequently has to be buried. Whence comes this life refusal? How does man become endowed with it? We do not know the answer to this. Religions have myths to explain its presence. The spiritual person is one who says that it is possible to become increasingly free of the power of anti-intentionality, and to root active life more and more in intentional action. This endeavour, he believes, is eminently worthwhile. It is in this that life's meaning is to be found. Thus knowledge of our own intentionality is concurrent with the degree of detachment that has been achieved. Contrariwise, self-knowledge is incompatible with attachment.

In the writings of the mystics there is a pattern. In the initial stages the ascetic's focus is upon the sensual object: sex, food, drink, or sleep, for instance. In the transition from asceticism to mysticism there is a recognition that essentially what needs to be mortified is self-love. An ascetic can abstain from sex, food, drink and sleep, but parade it before men. Jesus went out of his way to condemn the Pharisees for blowing their trumpets when they were giving alms. The implication here is that self-love is a sensual stroking of the self. It is appearance that is the motivating principle: how I appear to others is what motivates me to action. I am therefore 'in' another in that the other's approval is essential. I am in the power of the other, I am controlled by the other – but I also have to control the other so that he continues to stroke me. For this reason, the other has to be tailored inwardly to this image; the other is scooped into the role of stroking the self. The self is *in* the other and the other is *in* the self. This prevents an inner reality because the inner space is occupied by an outer figure.

The endeavour of the spiritual person is to detach the ego not from the desire for food, for drink, for sleep or for sex, but from that inflation of the ego that needs constant fuel. The fuel for this pseudo-power of the ego does not come from food but from greed, which is taking from others who are inwardly viewed with contempt. Greed consists in taking food that is unnecessary for bodily needs. It is taken for another motive – it caresses the bodily ego. There is an equation between being powerful and eating from the receptacle for others. That which is over and above the required amount represents others who are devoured, which gives an illusion of power. But the contempt of others becomes a contempt for the other-in-the-self. The self is damaged thereby, and then compensated for with illusory power.

The intentionality of psychic action cannot be ascertained when the intentional object is buried in a sensuous medium, be it sexual, erotic or sensual. What we have to determine is the nature of the intentional object.

The subject is conditioned by the state of the object. If the object is buried in a sensuous object, then the mind's subject is effected. The mind has to be created, or liberated, from the sensuous medium. The subject has the capacity for self-awareness but this is strangled if the intentional object is buried in the sensuous medium. The intentional object can be buried in the body, in a spouse, in two or three people. The subject is in the object and vice versa, so the subject's awareness of self is in proportion to the degree to which the intentional object is free of 'in-ness'. The state of the subject is determined by the state of the object. When the object is broken in pieces then this is the state of the subject. It is the state of the being of the intentional structure. If the intentional object is 'in' a sensual medium, then self-awareness and free thinking are absent. This is because the object is captive.

The intentional reality is structured into subject and object with a connection, but the subject is in the object and vice versa and the connection cannot exist without subject and object. The reality of the subject is the object and vice versa, but it is one being. The intentional structure supports itself. This is the ideal situation achieved only by few, the Buddha for example. There is a final battle with evil before this can occur.

The great mystics had a great showdown with evil, which personifies annihilation of the intentional structure. When the final detachment occurs the agent of self-destruction appears in all its nakedness. 'Throw yourself down', says Satan to Jesus, 'and God's angels will bear you up.' In other words, 'destroy yourself'. As said earlier the anxiety generated by this powerful agency is so strong that it is too much for normal mortals. This extreme anxiety is defended against by burying the intentional object 'in' sensuousness. But it is self-killing, spiritually and bodily.

There is a link between this self-killing and being 'in' the sensuous self-love. It is the suicide of the sort that Hermann Hesse describes in *Steppenwolf*:

> Among the common run of men there are many of little personality and stamped with no deep impress of fate, who find their end in suicide without belonging on that account to the type of suicide by inclination; while, on the other hand, of those who are to be counted as suicides by the very nature of their beings are many, perhaps a majority, who never in fact lay hands on themselves.

This sensuous self-image is the medium in which the intentional reality buries itself. It is because of its sensuous nature that the mind is clouded – it is therefore a death. Detachment is the liberation of the intentional reality from this imprisoning dungeon. The spiritual person is he whose central goal is this endeavour.

In traditional religion, the spiritual person detaches himself from sexual and erotic ties. This is the foundation stone from which he begins his spiritual work. It is therefore a work which is constructed on a base of isolation. This endeavour is undertaken in relation to his own self, which is his reference point. The other against which he measures himself are the writings of his spiritual ancestors, the counsel of a spiritual director.

Let us imagine a situation like this. A young man has left the world and entered a monastery. He prays earnestly, reads the scriptures, performs his spiritual duties, and examines his conscience each night. In this examination, he becomes aware of pride. In the Christian tradition this is the cardinal sin; the sin that poisons all virtues. 'If you are proud of being chaste', said St Aelred of Rievaulx, 'then it is a vice because pride is a vice.' So what does our young monk do to try and overcome it? He prays harder when he is bombarded with feelings of self-exaltation and does acts of penance. He discusses it with his spiritual director. He tries harder and harder, and yet in a moment of enlightenment he clearly sees that he has made no progress. The monk has a twin who is a Buddhist monk. He does not pray to a god because he does not believe in the deity. He also has a moment of enlightenment in which he realizes the presence of pride in himself, but he does not have the option of praying to God. What does he do? He strives harder, meditates more deeply and for longer hours, intensifies his ascetic practices, and consults regularly with his spiritual director. However, in this moment of enlightenment he knows that he is making no progress.

Both of them have reached a deadlock and they know it. Without a transformation, the situation has no resolution. Acts of restraint, attempts to be humble and so on are all to no avail because they feed an exalted self which remains unaffected. This is the condition of soul which today psychoanalysts call narcissism. Its solution cannot be found within the practices of traditional religion.

REFERENCES

Ernst Cassirer (1972) *An Essay on Man* (New Haven and London: Yale University Press), p. 5.
Hermann Hesse (1965) *Steppenwolf* (Harmondsworth: Penguin), p. 58.

21

Psychoanalysis – A Spirituality in the World

The moment that feeling ceases to be directed outwards, the moment it ceases to be an appreciation of the thing or the person with which it is connected in fact, it becomes unreal, or, to use a very appropriate term, sentimental.

(Macmurray, 1935)

Psychoanalysis is a morality functioning between persons bound together by familial or sexual intimacy. There is a sphere of activity existing between persons bound together by bonds of intimacy which we name the emotional. The emotional is the medium out of which the relationship is forged. If someone is physically cruel, he may beat the other with a whip. If he is emotionally cruel, he may treat the other with contempt. If I treat someone physically with contempt I push him aside. The emotional correlate of this is to push the person aside. The contemptuous action takes place in the communication flow between one person and another. The recipient of the action *feels* pushed aside by the other. He *is* pushed aside by the other. The action by which the other does this is according to an inner action pattern. The person who acts in this way does so according to an image.

Our baseline is that the subject does something and this doing is registered by the other in the feelings. The feelings are the psychological indicator of what is being done; they sift one action from another, and place an evaluation upon them. They are the registration chart of the things that are being done to the subject, and differentiate one action from another: I feel treated with contempt, I feel treated warily, I feel treated lovingly.

The feelings are the registration of the actions of the other. The actions of the other we call emotional. They are psychic actions which are real – we know they occur, that they have some bodily accompaniments. We do not

179

know how the action is transferred from one person to the other, but we do know that it happens. It is like the electric impulse that jumps from one terminal to the other across the intervening space.

There are emotional actions that differ widely from one another. A sample of the actions as quoted above is: contemptuous, wary, loving. I act contemptuously, I act warily, I act lovingly. Each of these adverbs sorts the actions into different categories. There is an exercise of judgement expressed in the adverb which is a moral one. Morality is defined according to actions towards the self or other on an axis of good or bad. The antonyms for the above adverbs would be: respectfully, trustingly, resentfully. This wide range of actions can be reduced to: good – lovingly, sympathetically, honestly; bad – resentfully, unsympathetically, dishonestly. It is not a question of whether people should judge in this way or not, but that they do. These emotional actions have moral tags attached to them. They are judged as they occur. They are judged by the recipient; the feeling is the judgement. Thus feelings are non-verbal judgements.

If the actions are different, then we have to ask, what is it about them that makes them different? We need to start by saying that the two general categories 'good' and 'bad' are different in kind. This basic difference is located in the source – the source of these two different kinds of action is different.

All actions are intentional in character and therefore flow from the ego. The ego, however, is not a unitary entity but is composed of fragments which can be in relation to one another or in antagonism to each other. Fragments in relation are the source of good actions, those in antagonism are the source of bad actions.

Relatedness is the inherent nature of the ego. It is possible, however, for a situation to arise where an opposition is set up to the ego's own nature as a consequence of pain. An intentional centrifugal flight of the fragments is set up instead of an intentional embrace – a centripetal movement. The intentional embrace brings the fragments of the ego into unison in enfolding the pain. These movements, or flows to embrace or to flee, are intentional in nature. However, flight anaesthetizes pain, so centripetal movement needs encouragement from outside. In the infantile situation we would see this encouragement as the emotional holding of the mother as described by Winnicott, or her containing function as described by

Bion. Intentional actions from fragments in centrifugal flight are judged bad; intentional actions from fragments in centripetal movement are judged good. Although one or the other can be aided from without, the ultimate determinant lies in choice as it is displayed in the fragments. Factors aiding centripetal movement could also lie in inherited disposition.

Bad emotional actions lead to mental illness, mental suffering, anti-social behaviour, depression, manic states, suicidal ideation, psychosis and neurosis. Patients suffering from one or more of the above conditions come to psychoanalysis in the hope of relief, which can only come if the actions that are bad are converted into good. Many an analysis only touches the surface and never reaches these currents of action which I have been trying to describe. Such analyses aim at symptom relief and are best named psychotherapy. However, if we follow Abraham in saying that the goal of psychoanalysis is the strengthening of character, then we must define such an analysis as having as its aim the transformation of bad actions into good; an analysis is successful to the extent that it is able to do this. In logic and in practice this transformation reduces the severity of mental illness, mental suffering, antisocial behaviour, depression, manic states, suicidal ideation, psychosis and neurosis.

If the goal of psychoanalysis is the transformation of bad actions into good, is it not right to call this a spiritual aim? An important focus of the analysts of the British School is the interpretation of omnipotence and envy. The reason for this is that both these conditions generate splitting, projection and concretization, and therefore are the progenitors of anxiety which lies at the base of mental illness. Mature religious principles also view omnipotence – usually called 'pride' in religious communities – and envy as evils to be rooted out. The motivation in the two is different: in religion, omnipotence and envy are considered bad in themselves; in psychoanalysis omnipotence and envy are the source of mental illness. However, in both traditions it is recognized that omnipotence and envy have negative consequences and are consequently destructive. The superficial view might be that they are considered bad in mature religions because they offend God, whereas in psychoanalysis it is because they are destructive to humans. I believe, however, that the idea that omnipotence and envy are bad because they are offensive to God is a view that is proper to primitive but not mature religion. God is not hurt or injured, which is a projection of a narcissistic ideation into the image of God.

In the Christian mythology there are two views of redemption which are profoundly different. One is that when Adam sinned, God was infinitely offended and sent his Son to make reparation for this offence. An infinite offence could only be repaired by a being who was infinite in nature equal in stature to the Father. This was seen as the rationale behind the redemption: it was centred on an offended God. The other view is that Adam's sin damaged humankind, and that the redemption was entirely for our sake, to repair the damage which had been done. In this view the whole religious effort is in the service of healing our damaged condition. This second view of redemption is both the Christian and the Judaic view. It is the authentic view of redemption, the one embodied in the New Testament, and elaborated in the writings of both the Greek and Latin fathers. It was only in the Middle Ages that the false view crept into theological thinking – another example of a degeneration of mature religion into primitive religion. The genuine view of redemption is one that is shared also by religions of the East. Seen from this perspective, Buddhism and Christianity have a joint aim. Whether God exists, as in Judaism or Christianity, or does not, as in Theravada Buddhism, does not matter because in each case there is a body of people who believe that omnipotence and envy are destructive, and therefore conditions of the soul to be healed.

Mature religion and psychoanalysis, then, have a joint goal: the conversion or transformation of actions which are destructive into actions which are constructive, or the transformation of actions which are bad into those which are good. The person who devotes his life to bringing about this transformation and doing so is spiritual. The person who decides to be psychoanalysed, who struggles with omnipotence and envy and has this as an important aim in his life, is also spiritual. However, the spiritual domain of religious people has been conscious, whereas the endeavour of those engaged in psychoanalysis is to tackle a sphere of the mind which is unconscious. If two different spheres of the mind are being addressed by these two traditions, we need to examine what these might be and how they differ.

When we turn our attention to spirituality we embark upon a very big subject. All the great religions have spawned schools of spirituality, each of which emphasizes a particular road to achieving spiritual maturity. Despite all these differences, certain keynotes are characteristic of all of them – so much so that the central means of achieving spiritual maturity are shared by spiritual schools in whatever religious tradition they are to be found. So, for instance, the spiritual aims of a Christian mystic, an Islamic Sufi, a Hasidic Jew, a Buddhist arahat or a Taoist saint will be and are very similar.

Psychoanalysis – a spirituality in the world

Psychoanalysis differs in that it is a spirituality in which there is no prayer. Instead, there is interpretation. Its sphere of attention is upon what is unconscious; this is its specifically designated area. Which area of psychic activity is unconscious? The answer to this is that it is those activities which are done *in phantasy*. These are actions which originate and are enacted in internal space. Their source is in the ego, and their object is that part of the personality which represents the external object world. The action affects the person or persons in the microsocial world. The effect upon the other occurs in his internal world, and the impact therefrom is registered in the feelings.

This imaginary life is the bridge that links one human being to another. The relationship is forged by the activity which we call 'actions in phantasy'. These actions arouse a cinema reel of images that are not necessarily consciously realized, but the feelings are stimulated, which are the judgements made upon the images. The images are not necessarily available to consciousness. This sphere of activity – the pouring fourth of images and feelings – we call the emotional. It is the sphere where unconsciousness frequently operates.

The sphere of action with which psychoanalysis is concerned is thus the emotional. It is particularly concerned with the moral actions which occur in this sphere. It is therefore a spirituality rooted at the most fundamental level of communication between human beings. As stated above, the actions at this level can either cause unease, dismay, terror or consternation, or create good feeling. When the parts of the self are in relation to one another, there is the creation of a good feeling; when the parts of the self are in antagonistic relation to one another, the result is bad feeling. Parts in relation to each other produce the good: parts in antagonism to each other produce the bad. When I speak of 'antagonistic relation', I mean the parts may be jammed up into each other, split apart from each other, and so on.

Parts in antagonism forswear knowledge, which is a product of parts in centripetal movement. A new piece of self-knowledge is a sign that parts have joined up, like two hydrogen atoms linking up to an oxygen atom to form a new entity. Consciousness is the product of parts in centripetal movement: unconsciousness is the result of parts in centrifugal movement. If this is correct and the aim of psychoanalysis is to make the unconscious conscious, then the aim can only be achieved through a transformation of centrifugal into centripetal movement. Consciousness and unconsciousness fluctuate according to the to-and-fro swaying of this inner movement between parts. Becoming conscious is a by-product of this transformation of inner movement, which comes about through

183

intentional decision. This swings the direction of the movement from one to the other.

When parts are in centripetal movement, there is a cohering ego whose actions are creative. Such action then creates good feeling. Emotions, then, are the actions of which the feelings are the registration. When the parts are in centrifugal movement, there is a dismembering of the ego and the actions perpetrate a range of bad feelings. The feelings are the good and bad judgements on these emotional actions, which are always moral, morality being that which is defined in terms of the good and bad.

As has been pointed out, spiritual endeavour aims at detachment from self-seeking in all its forms. Psychoanalysis is a spirituality, but thoroughly different in its methodology. The detachment is achieved through the agency of close emotional contact with another. The reason this works is as follows.

It is through the instrumentality of conscience that an individual deepens his spiritual development. Conscience raises its voice when the individual acts in a way that is damaging to himself. It is the psychological correlate to pain, with the difference that whereas pain is experienced subsequent to a physical injury, conscience raises its voice when the subject is preparing to act. The damaging act itself can only be done by silencing conscience. Conscience is the signal that there is danger lurking to the psychological self. Emotional actions that are below the threshold of awareness can either build up the health of the person, in other words be integrative, or be destructive. As it is below the threshold of awareness, we need an indicator to help us know whether an action is integrative or destructive.

Emotional actions only become knowable in the sphere of emotional intimacy. A cardinal principle in psychoanalysis is that the analyst represents the emotional core of the patient. This is the transference. From this the analyst is able to make the inference that what is being done emotionally to him in this closely confined emotional situation is an exact register of what is being done to the patient's self. With the use of this inference, the analyst is able to make clear to the patient the nature of his emotional actions. This enables the patient, through slow painful struggle, to purify his emotional activity.

The diversity of emotional activity only comes into being when an individual is brought into emotional intimacy with another. In a state of emotional isolation, the emotions are frozen and therefore cannot be known. The analytic situation is not only one where the analyst reveals to the patient the character of his emotional actions, but the very situation itself brings these actions into being. The analytic situation is an emotional catalyst. Psychoanalysis has brought to the spiritual endeavour a knowledge of inner parts of the self and their manner of interacting. This was not scientifically known in the traditional religions.

REFERENCE

John Macmurray (1935) *Freedom in the Modern World* (London: Faber & Faber), p. 151.

22

Science and Religion

Determinism is always reappearing in new forms since it satisfies a deep human wish: to give up, *to get rid of freedom, responsibility, remorse, all sorts of personal individual unease, and surrender to fate and the relief of 'it could not be otherwise'.*

(Murdoch, 1993)

In the model of the mind which has been adopted by mature religions, the individual has freedom of choice, ultimately between the good and the bad. This is the libertarian view of the mind. There is a consequence to this choice: in Christianity there is a judgement, and the individual goes either to heaven or to hell; in Buddhism the individual is reborn either into a higher level of life or into a lower level. The individual is judged according to the life choices that he has made.

There is another model which is determinist: what I do is determined by antecedent causes, and therefore I have no choice. I am determined by forces outside my control. This model is in direct opposition to the religious model. The determinist model has become identified with science. This identification, however, is based on false premises.

Science is an attitude of mind which seeks to verify beliefs. There is an oscillation between observation of phenomena and beliefs. It is prepared to overthrow a belief and replace it with another should observation prove that the belief is incorrect. In scientific language, a belief is called a hypothesis. It is inherent in the definition of a hypothesis that it is susceptible to change. In this it differs from a religious belief as religious belief organizes the data of experience according to a particular pattern that is unalterable. In religion the data of experience are moulded to fit the patterning of belief; in science the hypothesis is altered to fit the data of experience.

Philosophically there is a third position falling between these two which is that although man chooses, these choices are determined. Sometimes 'reconciliationists' are known as 'soft determinists'. This third view is nevertheless determinist. There are then two main models of the mind: the determinist and the libertarian. Mature religions have adopted the libertarian hypothesis, whereas the agnostic or atheistic schools of thought have adopted the determinist one. This is not hard and fast: for instance, in some of the contemporary attempts by the Christian churches to be 'relevant' to the modern world the determinist hypothesis has been adopted. Also, certain thinkers who are agnostic or atheist have adopted the libertarian hypothesis.

The question of which of these two hypotheses is scientific is to be determined not by evangelistic enterprise but by a slow process of comparing each with the data of experience. The fact that the libertarian hypothesis has been so widely adopted by mature religions neither makes it true nor untrue, and that the determinist view has been so enthusiastically adopted by the sons of the Enlightenment is no guarantee of its scientific validity. Traditional religion has become associated, not without good reason, with prejudice, superstition and dogmatism against which educated scientists have revolted with vehement protest.

Freud belonged to a scientific group which constituted just such a protest. He was a pupil of Ernst Brücke, who was a foundation member of the Berliner Physicalische Gesellschaft. The four founders were passionately opposed to any form of vitalism, the belief that living organisms were animated by a soul or a special principle. Psychoanalysis, then, has grown up in the shadow of this determinist model, and has been guided by its principles.

The libertarian hypothesis accords better with the data of experience. This is not the sort of hypothesis that can be proved by deductive logic, but only through 'convergence of probabilities'. To prove it through a wide-ranging survey of the findings of the human sciences is beyond my competence. I intend to bring forth just one datum of experience culled from the consulting-room. I shall give some examples of the phenomenon, and then abstract the common thread and the deduction that I make of it.

A woman came to me in distress because her boyfriend had become sexually impotent; as he was about to make love to her he lost his erection. This had occurred with previous boyfriends on two occasions, and she was anxious about it, meaning she might have something to do with it. Three sessions passed in which she told me of her family background and other matters. Towards the end of the third session, I was about to make an interpretation, but as I was about to put it into speech it faded from my mind. I noted it and pondered on the equivalence between this and her boyfriend's detumesced penis. In the next session, the same thing happened again. I focused my psychic attention upon this phenomenon, and in the next session an interpretation began to crystallize in my mind. I put my energies into putting it into speech and delivering it to her, which I did. The following session she came in with a smile on her face and told me that her boyfriend had last night been able to make love to her. She felt that the explanation for this success lay in the last session she had had with me. She believed, therefore, that something she had taken from the session had favoured her boyfriend's sexual potency.

A woman was exploited at work by her boss. He kept her at work beyond her contractual hours, made her work during her lunch hour, and spoke to her disrespectfully. She did not pay me a proper fee; she used to go on speaking so I was not able to finish the session on time; when I made an interpretation she would ignore what I had said. One session I pointed all this out to her. She paused and said through gritted teeth, 'Perhaps you're right'. The following day she said to me that her boss had been quite unlike he had ever been before.

These examples demonstrate that the individual is instrumental in constructing his or her microsocial environment. The sexual, emotional or social response depends upon the mode of the individual's construction. The microsocial environment is not a given but a construction. The individual constructs one response or another. The emotional environment is conditioned by choice. My experience is that the libertarian model fits the data of experience that are daily culled in the consulting-room, or are capable of being so culled.

My conclusion is that the libertarian hypothesis is scientific, i.e., that it is verified by psychoanalysis in the intrapsychic and interpersonal field, and that the determinist hypothesis is disproved. On this basis I would wish to argue further that psychoanalysis is impoverished through operating on the determinist hypothesis, and that it needs to be restructured in its theoretical outlook and replaced with the libertarian hypothesis.

It might be argued that as long as the clinical work is being done in a satisfactory manner it does not matter if the theory which supports it is out of kilter with the practical work. There are two arguments which I should like to bring up in opposition to this. The first is that a theory, if it is to be of use, needs to be generated by the practical clinical work that is being done, otherwise it hinders conceptualization. The determinist theory was laid down by Freud because this was his philosophical outlook which he inherited from the Berliner Physicalische Gesellschaft. It was also the philosophical position held almost exclusively by the scientific establishment in the nineteenth century. There were a few exceptions, like Franz Brentano, but they were regarded as cranks.

The determinist model was imported on the basis of a prejudice, not because it had been tested against the clinical data. Freud was great enough to refuse to twist his clinical data beyond a certain point, instead over the years changing his model so that it moved ever closer to the libertarian model, but he never relinquished the determinist model, which was to the detriment of psychoanalysis. Psychoanalysts who have followed Freud have also maintained this model of the mind. A good theory – a theory which assists the clinician in grappling with his practical work – is one which has been formulated from the clinical experience. The genius of Freud was his acute clinical insight, but this was hampered by the determinist theory. This continues to be the case.

The second reason why discordant theory affects clinical practice is that it robs the analyst of conviction. I say 'the analyst', but the same applies in any situation where the human being is being guided by a discordant theory. If the person believes the theory, but his practice is at variance with the theory, then he is split in his affective relations to objects. In the example of the analyst, it means that there is a partial identification with the supplier of the theory and another part which is engaged in the discourse with the patient. It means that there is a part of the analyst which is not engaged in the discourse. The point I am trying to make can be looked at from another angle. It is from the experience of the person who rejects a discordant theory and adopts one which fits his own interpersonal experience with the patient. The analyst experiences an illumination, a moment of personal insight; this is followed by personal conviction that comes from a personal act of understanding. This is a different state of mind from when he was in discord from his theory, when he was split. An integrated mind whose subjective expression is conviction interacts quite differently with his patients from someone without personal conviction. An analyst in possession of such a state of mind speaks from his heart to the heart of the patient. For both these reasons it matters profoundly that the theory marries up with the practice.

Because there is such a deep-seated prejudice that the determinist model is scientific whereas the libertarian model is not, psychoanalysis has embraced the determinist model with fervour. Psychoanalytic societies have such a fear of not being scientific that they dare not embrace a model which has been mostly the preserve of religion. The fact that traditional religion has been rife with superstition and dogmatism does not imply that all its philosophical assumptions are wrong. We witness a phenomenon which has occurred often in the history of ideas: that because a tradition is full of bad ideas the whole is ditched. It has been a commonplace of traditional religion that there has been a violent repudiation of attempts to validate beliefs through the production of evidence. However, the presumption that the libertarian hypothesis is therefore a product of superstition is an unwarranted prejudice. The antagonism on the part of the human sciences towards dogmatic beliefs barraged against scientific investigation is all too welcome. This, however, does not justify its own unscientific repudiation of the libertarian hypothesis. It is my view that psychoanalysis, like many of its sister disciplines in the human sciences, has embraced the determinist hypothesis with the same dogmatism with which religions cling to their doctrines. In other words, psychoanalysis has not tested one of its most baseline theories: the determinist hypothesis. In fact, it has shown the same adamant refusal to test it scientifically as its enemy, the traditional religions.

In the same way, traditional religions have taken up a prejudiced attitude towards psychoanalysis. This is partly because of its aggressively atheistic stance, but it is also because psychoanalysis has been able to uncover greed, envy, jealousy, pride and hatred in a sphere that is vital for modern man, and in which traditional religions have had no access. Psychoanalysis has been far more successful in uncovering the vices in the emotional sphere than any of the traditional religions. This is because it has adopted a scientific method of investigating this sphere and has developed it to levels of considerable sophistication. Psychoanalysis, then, has robbed from traditional religions a portion of its own care of souls and has developed an understanding of the psyche never attained by pastors, rabbis or religious teachers.

The psychoanalytic method is one which both uncovers the emotional currents, vicious and virtuous, in the individual psyche and at the same time scientifically traces their origin and connections. Freud developed psychoanalysis because he believed that if it were possible to observe the structure of a neurosis then he could gain power over it. There is another way of looking at this which fits well with the thesis of this book: when an individual can see clearly his or her vicious emotions, there is an option: either to stop seeing, or to stop doing. It is again the principle of Socrates that you cannot do something vicious and know it at the same time. You cannot know and do; if you see the doing, you cannot do. The psychoanalytic method is able to reveal what is being done, and this is done scientifically. The patient has a response which can also be traced scientifically – the scientific and therapeutic pathways travel along in tandem.

My conclusion is that psychoanalysis is a spiritual activity, but at the same time it is scientific and in this way it is different from traditional spiritualities. It is a spirituality appropriate to our scientific age.

REFERENCE

Iris Murdoch (1993) *Metaphysics as a Guide to Morals* (London: Allen Lane The Penguin Press), p. 190.

Conclusion

A patient comes to the analyst because he is suffering mental pain. He is suffering because he is doing something that brings about the mental pain, but he does not know what it is that he does. The reason he comes to the analyst is to be relieved of his suffering. The analyst cannot take it away, but through interpretation the patient can come to know himself and begin to construct his inner and outer world anew. In the process of reconstruction, the activity which was the source of suffering changes. Constructive action replaces destructive action.

The message that lies at the heart of mature religion is that constructive emotional action is what gives meaning to our lives. In constructive emotional action the freedom of the other is respected as well as the reality of my own self. It is love that respects the freedom and reality of the other. Therefore, although he does not know it, when a patient wants to be relieved of his mental suffering, he desires to put value where it had not existed before. Placing this value as the goal of emotional action is a spiritual act.

It is not recognized as a spiritual act either by traditional religion or by psychoanalysis. This action, although extremely simple, lies at the heart of all close emotional relations, and traditional religions do not have knowledge of it. Psychoanalysis, on the other hand, does have knowledge of those states of mind that generate destructive emotional action, but has been fearful to name the constructive desire.

Psychoanalysis is, I believe, a mature natural religion. This is a very radical statement. Psychoanalysis has, I believe, degenerated because it has reneged upon its radical character and allowed itself to become domesticated. When it is not watered down, psychoanalysis is a very radical phenomenon in our world. This book is an attempt to replace it where it belongs.

Index

Index

Index

Winnicott, Donald   72, 73, 86–7, 88,
   115, 120, 180
wish-fulfilment   68

Yahuda, Abraham Shalom   63

Yahweh, human attributes   23

Zahn, Gordon   79, 83
Zarathustra   14, 17–18, 22–3, 30
Zilboorg, Gregory   90–2, 93, 96